A NEW OWNER'S
GUIDE TO
CHINESE CRESTEDS

JG-124

Overleaf: A Chinese Crested adult and puppy photographed by Isabelle Francais.

Opposite Page: One of the world's few modern hairless dogs, the Chinese Crested is perhaps the most handsome of the hairless breeds.

The Publisher wishes to acknowledge the following owners of the dogs in this book: Arlene Butterklee, Jean C. Edwards, Patricia Franklin, Victor Helu, Pamela Litz, Michael Lucero, Joseph and Phyllis Rachunas, Linda G. Tamar, Dottie Thompson, Jackie Wendelkin.

Photographers: Alverson Photographers, Mary Bloom, Booth Photography, Tara Darling, Isabelle Francais, Bruce and Jean Harkins, Kurtis Photography, Standard Image Photography.

The author acknowledges the contribution of Judy Iby for the following chapters: Sport of Purebred Dogs, Identification and Finding the Lost Dog, Traveling With Your Dog, Health Care, Behavior and Canine Communication.

The portrayal of canine pet products in this book is for is for general instructive value only; the appearance of such products does not necessarily constitute an endorsement by the authors, the publisher, or the owners of the dogs portrayed in this book.

© by T.F.H. Publications, Inc.

Distributed in the UNITED STATES to the Pet Trade by T.F.H. Publications, Inc., One T.F.H. Plaza, Neptune City, NJ 07753; on the Internet at www.tfh.com; in CANADA Rolf C. Hagen Inc., 3225 Sartelon St. Laurent-Montreal Quebec H4R 1E8; Pet Trade by H & L Pet Supplies Inc., 27 Kingston Crescent, Kitchener, Ontario N2B 2T6; in ENGLAND by T.F.H. Publications, PO Box 15, Waterlooville PO7 6BQ; in AUSTRALIA AND THE SOUTH PACIFIC by T.F.H. (Australia), Pty. Ltd., Box 149, Brookvale 2100 N.S.W., Australia; in NEW ZEALAND by Brooklands Aquarium Ltd. 5 McGiven Drive, New Plymouth, RD1 New Zealand; in SOUTH AFRICA, Rolf C. Hagen S.A. (PTY.) LTD. P.O. Box 201199, Durban North 4016, South Africa; in Japan by T.F.H. Publications, Japan—Jiro Tsuda, 10-12-3 Ohjidai, Sakura, Chiba 285, Japan. Published by T.F.H. Publications, Inc.

MANUFACTURED IN THE
UNITED STATES OF AMERICA
BY T.F.H. PUBLICATIONS, INC.

A New Owner's
Guide to
Chinese Cresteds

Joseph Rachunas

Contents

1998 Edition

The Chinese Crested is available in several colors, and can be either solid or spotted.

Both hairless and coated dogs can be found within the same litter of Chinese Cresteds.

The Chinese Crested's eyes are almond shaped and set wide apart.

Good breeders only raise litters from parents that are free of genetic disorders.

Good manners are paramount, but appearance and grooming are all important too.

INTRODUCTION to the Chinese Crested Dog

My Chinese Cresteds, Mati and Ausie, where have you been all my life? No, they are not as old as I am, but for the 20-plus years that I've been showing my Afghan Hounds, I subconsciously have been looking for the perfect breed for my lifestyle. I still love my Afghans and would not part with them for the world, but Chinese Cresteds have found a special place in my heart. Next to my marriage to Phyllis and our children, the Cresteds are the best things that have happened to me.

I felt I was somewhat knowledgeable about Afghans, but going into a new breed, especially the Crested, posed several problems. First, there is not as much information available on this breed as there is on other breeds. So, I began with the purchase of the only book on the Crested that I could find, and ended with exorbitant telephone bills for several months until I bought my first Crested. My quest for information is of course, ongoing. My wife and I met and talked with several great people who own Cresteds, from whom we gleaned our basic knowledge. Many thanks to these individuals for their patience and indulgence.

I feel very strongly that the lovers of the Crested are growing in number. This is attested to by the soaring increase in entries, from about 50 in 1993 to over 200 at the 1997 National Specialty. That is a 400% increase! The American Chinese Crested Club (ACCC) is confident that this will prove to be just the beginning after a somewhat meager (in comparison to today's record entries), slow and arduous start. The first annual Specialty Show, in which 33 Cresteds were shown, was held in Baltimore, Maryland by the now parent organization, the ACCC, on June 1, 1980. The ACCC members' perseverance and hard missionary work are definitely paying off now and showing signs of fruition.

It is my hope that this publication, in some small way, assists and fosters the breed's growth by helping the novice to appreciate the wonderful world of the Chinese Crested. There is more to that world than just acquiring a dog. For the experience to be successful and mutually rewarding, it is essential that you know how and be willing to properly care for this unique canine companion. This book addresses some of the information you will need to provide for that care. Whether you are interested in showing your Crested or just having it as your special little loving companion, this book will help you develop and sustain a long and bountiful relationship.

This publication is a compilation of the information that I found of great interest, especially because I knew nothing about the Crested and started from ground zero. Interspersed are some of my experiences as an Afghan owner and breeder that I believe relate to the Crested. Some of you "old hands" may find it of interest as well.

The popularity of the Chinese Crested—whether Hairless or Powderpuff—is on the rise—and for good reason!

HISTORY of the Chinese Crested Dog

The story of how the Chinese Crested actually originated has virtually been lost over the centuries. It is thought that hairless dogs existed as long ago as 2000 to 1000 BC. Through archaeological evidence such as statues, pottery, paintings, engravings and carvings, historians have been able to confirm the existence of hairless dogs in Africa, Turkey, Portugal, Indies, Mexico, Central and South America, China and the Philippines.

Pottery artifacts believed to date to 1000 BC have been found in diggings in central and southern Mexico. It is believed that what is now known as the Chinese Crested evolved from the African Hairless.

The first hairless dogs are believed to have arrived in China during the Han Dynasty (202 BC–AD 220). The Chinese, who preferred smaller dogs, may have bred to reduce the dogs to a "toy" size. A pre-Aztec culture in the Toltes period (900–1200 AD) held the small hairless dogs in reverence. The dogs were believed to represent perfect and unselfish love (a trait that today's owners will attest seems to have endured). These dogs were buried with their masters in tribute to the masters' good deeds. The Aztecs later abandoned the hairless dogs as a spiritual image and instead ate them as sacred food on special occasions.

Statues and paintings depicting hairless dogs were uncovered in the tombs of Egyptian pharaohs. People of that era believed that the hairless dog possessed mystical healing powers. They were revered by everyone, but owned only by the elite.

In the 1400s and 1500s, Spanish explorers found hairless dogs in Mexico as well as in other parts of South and Central America. The missionaries, who frequently accompanied the Spanish explorers, recorded sightings of various dogs, some of which were hairless and resembled the Chinese Crested. These dogs were also used in trade. It is thought that hairless dogs—very possibly ancestors of the Crested—were brought back to Spain as the sailors returned home. During the course of the long voyage, some of the dogs may have been used for food. Thankfully, some also survived.

The Vatican owns several paintings of street scenes that show hairless dogs during the Roman Empire. In the 15th century painting *Christ Nailed to the Cross*, artist Gerad David depicts a small hairless dog with a crest, socks and a tail with a plume.

There is no true recorded history of the Chinese Crested prior to the late 1700s, when the breed was included in a book about dogs. This book included a print of what was called the Chinese Hairless Dog. French, British and Portuguese explorers reported finding the hairless dogs in parts of Africa and Asia in the 1700s and 1800s.

Two fine-looking spotted Chinese Cresteds. The Chinese Crested is available in several colors, including pink, black, mahogany, blue, lavender, and copper; it can be solid or spotted.

In the 1850s and 1860s a well-known English dog fancier and show judge, Mr. W. K. Taunton, collected rare breeds of dog during his world travels. His collection of Chinese Cresteds included a Hairless that he named Chinese Emperor. He later exhibited the Emperor in 1897. Other judges of the era were not as impressed with the Crested as Taunton was, and felt that the dogs should be kept only as pets and companions. The Hairless was considered a curiosity item and was exhibited in London's Zoological Gardens. Mr. Taunton is also responsible for importing the first Afghan Hound, called Motee, to Great Britain. The Crested is believed to be a close relative of the Afghan Hound as their body structure, and even their temperaments, are somewhat alike.

The hairless dogs were called by several names that referred to the countries in which they were found. In China they were called the Chinese Hairless, Chinese Ship Dog, Chinese Royal Hairless and Chinese Edible Dog. Africans knew the breed as the South African Hairless. In Turkey they were the Turkish Hairless; in Egypt the Giza Hairless. The "toy" Chinese Crested has been confused with other hairless dogs, which in some cases were larger than a toy size, such as the Mexican Hairless, Inca Orchid, Turkish Greyhound, African Elephant Dog, Indian Rampur Dog, Abyssinian Sand Dog, Buenos Aires Dog and Xoloitzcuintli (pronounced show-lo-eets-quintli or shortened to simply Xolo).

The most profitable mode of travel on the commonly used trade routes was by ship. The Chinese were renowned sailors who sailed the seas for centuries and who are given credit for introducing the hairless dog into a number of countries through their travels. This may be why hairless dogs seems to be more prevalent in port cities.

The hairless dogs were found to serve a vital purpose during the plagues—the curse of the Middle Ages. Nature provides for both the curse and the cure; the bad and the good. In this case, the negative was the ravage of nature and the terrible loss of human life caused by the plague, and the positive was the development and the advancement of the hairless dog for a specific purpose.

The Bubonic Plague, known as the Black Death, devastated Europe and Asia in the 14th century. The plague was transmitted by fleas carrying bacterium from infected rats. It became imperative that the ships' crews rid the sailing ships of all rats prior to leaving port, because the presence of even a single rat meant almost certain death at sea. The hairless dogs were enlisted to aid the crews in the life and death struggle to rout out any of the vermin that may have been on board. The fact that the dogs were hairless made it easy to detect the presence of any fleas. Once detected, the fleas could be picked off and destroyed, and thus the

The Chinese Crested occurs in both varieties, the Hairless and the coated, or Powderpuff.

The popularity of the Chinese Crested has flourished since it was reinstated to the AKC in 1986.

hairless dogs became integral and essential members of the crews.

ESTABLISHING A FOUNDATION

During a chance meeting with AKC Judge Mitchell T. Wooden of North Hollywood, California, he related to me that he had several occasions to visit with Gypsy Rose Lee at her home. Purportedly, the famous burlesque star had 17 Chinese Cresteds, all of whom were Hairless and look-a-likes in size, color and furnishings.

Gypsy Rose acquired her first Crested from her sister June Havoc in the early '50s and went on to play an integral role in the history of the breed. Gypsy exported her dogs to England and other countries, helping to establish the foundation of the Chinese Crested breed.

AMERICAN KENNEL CLUB (AKC) RECOGNITION

The first official record of a Chinese Crested being shown was April 28 to May 1, 1885, where a Crested was exhibited under the auspices of the Westminster Kennel Club in the Miscellaneous Class at the ninth annual New York bench show. However, the exact dates of the following sequence of events remain unknown.

Mrs. Ida Garrett, a newspaperwoman from New York City, became interested in hairless dogs—especially the Chinese Crested—in the 1800s. She promoted, bred and exhibited the dogs for over 60 years. In 1920 she assisted Mrs. Debra Woods in obtaining several hairless breeds, including the Crested. The two women jointly promoted the Crested for nearly 40 years.

In the 1930s Mrs. Woods began to keep a log of her dogs, which eventually escalated into a registry service of all hairless dogs. Mrs. Woods, owner of the Crest Haven Kennels in Florida, founded the American Hairless Dog Club (AHDC) in 1959. The registry was maintained and closely guarded by Mrs. Woods for another ten years until her death in 1969. Mrs. Paul J. (Mary Lou) Orlik of Norfolk, Virginia, who was the corresponding secretary of AHDC, purchased the Crest Haven Kennels, including the registry. This registry service was maintained by the Orliks for nearly 12 years until the American Chinese Crested Club (ACCC) was founded in October 1978, at which time the club became the owner of the registry.

The Crested was eligible to be shown in the Miscellaneous Class from 1955 to 1965. In 1965, the AKC made the breed ineligible to be exhibited because entries were so low, but the decision was also due to the facts that there was no specialty (parent) club to support the breed and there were no official breed standards. After the formation of the ACCC, some time passed before the Crested was once again permitted to be exhibited in the Miscellaneous Class; this occurred February 1, 1986. At that time there were two sets of standards in use: one for the Hairless and one for the Powderpuff.

The Miscellaneous Class is used by the AKC as sort of a "holding area" until the particular breed has recognizable nationwide support. Admission to the AKC Stud Book requires clear and categorical proof that a substantial, sustained nationwide interest and participation exists for the breed. Included in this requirement is an active parent club with serious and expanding breeding activity nationwide. The breeds in the Miscellaneous Class may compete in AKC obedience trials and earn obedience titles. They may also compete in conformation shows, but are limited to the Miscellaneous Class (no Group competition) and cannot earn championship points. If the breed shows continuing health and growth, it may be given Stud Book status by the Board of Directors of the AKC, and may then compete in the regular classes for championship points.

On June 12, 1990 the AKC approved a new standard for the Chinese Crested. The standard, which is applicable to both the Hairless and the Powderpuff varieties by the direction of the AKC, was presented by the ACCC. The standard was the culmination of hundreds of hours of arduous work by many members of the ACCC.

The Chinese Crested became eligible for AKC registration on February 1, 1991. The first Crested to be registered was *Ch. Conversation Piece N'Co is pictured winning Best of Opposite Sex at the Kalamazoo Kennel Club in 1995.* Maya of Rivercrest, registration number D413100. On April 1st of that same year, the Crested (Hairless and Powderpuff) became eligible to be shown at AKC-licensed events in the Toy Group.

STANDARD of the Chinese Crested Dog

ebster's New World Dictionary defines standard as: • Something established for use as a rule or basis of comparison in measuring or judging capacity, quantity, content, extent, value, quality, etc. • A level of excellence, attainment, etc. regarded as a measure of adequacy. • Applies to some measure, principle, model, etc. with which things of the same class are compared in order to determine their quantity, value, quality, etc. Criterion applies to a test or rule for measuring the excellence, fitness, or correctness of something.

As you can see, even Webster could not quite nail down what a standard is; he can explain what it does, but not what it is. That is why a standard is prone to individual interpretation—accurate or not, right or wrong—it is not absolute. Although there is one AKC standard to adhere to, interpretations of the standard for the Crested vary by geographic locations, likes and dislikes and what is "in" at any point in time.

Ch. Winsalot Maiden Chyna winning 1994 Best of Breed or Variety at the Starved Rock Kennel Club show.

Standards are man-made and as such are subject to change. The human species is always attempting to fool with Mother Nature and as man made changes have occurred, the standard for the Chinese Crested has changed as well. At this point, no one can say with any degree of absolute certainty what the original Crested looked like, but please let's not adulterate the beauty that nature created any more than we have already.

The current standard for the Crested was approved June 12, 1990 by the AKC and became effective April 1, 1991. The official standard is cited section by section, and following each section is an explanation of that part of the standard in italics. The explanation is part of an illustrated guide produced by the AKC with the cooperation of the ACCC as part of the Judge's Guide.

OFFICIAL AKC STANDARD FOR THE CHINESE CRESTED

General Appearance—A toy dog, fine-boned, elegant and graceful. The distinct varieties are born in the same litter. The Hairless with hair only on the head, tail and feet and the Powderpuff, completely covered with hair. The breed serves as a loving companion, playful and entertaining.

The Chinese Crested is not too fine-boned as to appear spindly nor too heavy-boned as to appear bulky. He presents a balanced, graceful picture.

Size, Proportion, Substance—*Size*—Ideally 11 to 13 inches. However, dogs that are slightly larger or smaller may be given full consideration.

Proportion—rectangular—proportioned to allow for freedom of movement. Body length from withers to base of tail is slightly longer than the height at the

Multiple Group winner Ch. Cryptonite N'Co winning Best of Breed or Variety at the 1995 Oakland County Kennel Club.

CCCN
RESERVE WINNERS

Ch. Xu Fei Sanuchar Bart O Wimbar, 1995 Reserve Winners Dog at the Chinese Crested Club of Nashville Show.

withers. **Substance**—Fine-boned and slender but not so refined as to appear breakable or alternatively, not a robust, heavy structure.

Type and soundness are more important than size. A dog that presents a correct picture of a Crested is to be given equal consideration even if slightly over or under the indicated size range. The Crested's rectangular proportion allows for the smooth flowing gait. The Crested is a slender dog, without being overly narrow. He is not delicate or fragile, but is graceful. He is neither cobby nor stocky. Anything resembling dwarfism is incorrect.

Head—Expression—Alert and intense.

This is not a head breed. Overall appearance is most important. The Chinese Crested is quite aware of what happens around him and is usually quite interested in his surroundings. His expression, due to the wide placement of the eyes, is rather soft and sweet. When the Crested is alert there is a lot of sparkle in his expression.

17

The Chinese Crested's eyes are almond shaped and set wide apart. The lighter-colored dogs may have lighter-colored eyes, and darker-colored dogs have dark eyes.

Eyes—Almond-shaped, set wide apart. Dark-colored dogs have dark-colored eyes, and lighter-colored dogs may have lighter-colored eyes. Eye rims match the coloring of the dog.

The eyes should not be too large, too round or too prominent. Eyes should not be set too close. Lighter-colored dogs may have lighter colored eyes. The eye rims, in matching with the dog's coloration, especially in the Hairless variety, may be spotted or may be light, as in a pink or lavender dog, matching the rest of the dog's skin. Eye faults— Set too close. Round eye. Set too wide.

Ears—Uncropped large and erect, placed so that the base of the ear is level with the outside corner of the eye.

The actual angle of the ear set is not specified, just as long as the lower edge of the base of the ear is even with the outside corner of the eye. Therefore some dogs can have a rather high ear carriage and it is still correct. When very alert, some Cresteds' ears can come up so close as to almost touch (complete with wrinkles in the top of the head) and this is not a fault. Ears set too low are seen more frequently than those set too high. Nothing is said as to whether the ear is triangular and pointed, or more rounded (as the English ear), only that it must be erect. Both are correct. A rosed, tipped or dropped ear is incorrect. Ear faults—Set too low. Set too high. Hooded.

Ch. Sanuchar Kaus of Xu Fei with owner Pat Franklin winning Waukesha Kennel Club's 1995 Winners Dog title.

Skull—The skull is arched gently over the occiput from ear to ear. Distance from the occiput to stop equal to distance from stop to tip of nose. The head is wedge-shaped viewed from above and the side.

The skull has a slight curve from ear to ear and is not round and domey. The muzzle is ideally equal in length from tip of nose to stop and from stop to occiput, but many are slightly shorter and very pretty. A broad, square muzzle or a really short one, whether broad or "foxy," is less desirable. The wedge-shaped head should give a clean blended appearance.

Stop—Slight but distinct.

The stop is not so exaggerated as that of a Chihuahua, but is definitely more than that of a Collie. It can be seen and felt, but it is not very deep. Placing your thumb into the stop should allow you to feel a slight blend into the skull.

Muzzle—Cheeks taper cleanly into the muzzle.

Cheeks should not be pouchy, but flat and clean. The muzzle should not look "tacked-on." The line from the tip of the nose to the base of the ear is smooth.

Nose—Dark in dark-colored dogs; may be lighter in lighter-colored dogs. Pigment is solid.

Due to the wide range of color in this breed, the variation of dark-colored as well as lighter-colored dogs can be great. In dark-colored dogs, the nose is usually black or dark brown, the brown being the brown or beige-toned dogs. It can be self-colored on the light dogs. The nose must be a solid color.

Lips—Lips are clean and tight. The Crested has no flews.

Bite—Scissors or level in both varieties. Missing teeth in the Powderpuff are to be faulted. The Hairless variety is not to be penalized for absence of full dentition.

Ch. Winsalot Ausker D'Dasa winning a Group Two placement at the Belle City Kennel Club Show in 1995.

In the Hairless variety, bites should be given equal consideration against other Hairless and Powderpuffs. Along with missing teeth, the Hairless may also have crooked ones, especially a tusk-like canine. The gums must still be lined up in a scissors or even position. Hairless may have teeth that are shaped differently in that they are more pointed and narrower. They almost look like puppy teeth.

Neck, Topline, Body—*Neck*—Neck is lean and clean, slightly arched from the withers to the base of the skull and carried high. *Topline*—Level to slightly sloping croup. *Body*—Brisket extends to the elbow. Breastbone is not prominent. Ribs are well developed. The depth of the chest tapers to a moderate tuck-up at the flanks. Light in loin.

To achieve the proper arch of the neck, a certain amount of length is necessary. Cresteds, when at attention, tend to arch their necks slightly more than is required. A short, stocky, "bull" neck is incorrect. The neck should blend into the shoulders and topline. The layback of the shoulder slopes into a level back, which, in turn,

The skin of the Chinese Crested is an important feature: it is fine-grained and smooth. In the Powderpuff variety, the coat consists of a soft veil of long hair.

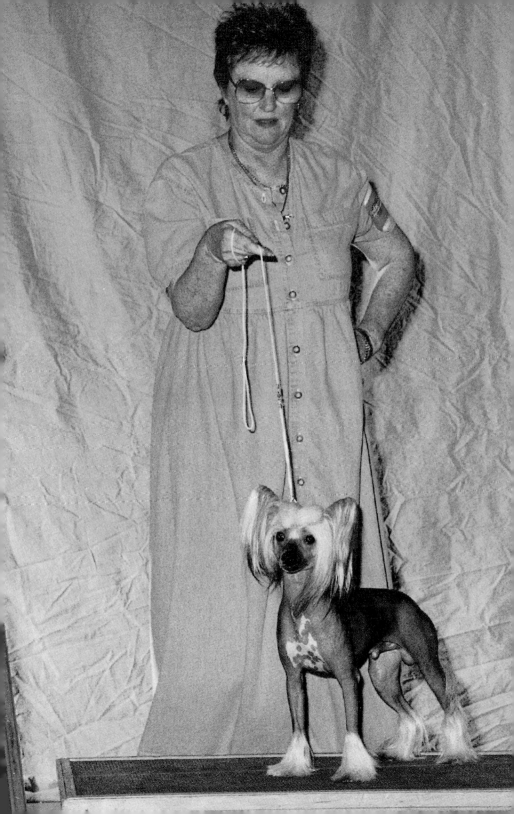

rounds off by sloping gently into a slight croup. The croup lowers the tail set slightly. Cresteds need enough substance and depth of body so they do not appear spindly. Cresteds are neither slab-sided nor barrel-shaped in the ribs. They are smooth and well-developed but not overdone, with a tuck-up and a lighter loin area.

Tail—Tail is slender and tapers to a curve. It is long enough to reach the hock. When dog is in motion, the tail is carried gaily and may be carried slightly forward over the back. At rest the tail is down with a slight curve upward at the end resembling a sickle. In the Hairless variety, two-thirds of the end of the tail is covered by long, flowing feathering referred to as a plume. The Powderpuff variety's tail is completely covered with hair.

The Chinese Crested's shoulders and elbows are not so tight as to restrict its movement, nor are they floppy and loose.

The Crested's tail is usually hock-length. In motion the tail is usually out or up and may be carried over the back. At rest the tail usually drops. It should not be tucked, although the bravest Hairless will tuck when cold. They get cold easily in wind, air-conditioning, etc. The plume may be long with a long, full crest or less so with a sparser crest. The Powderpuff's tail is covered with hair and may plume or feather.

Forequarters—*Angulation*— Layback of shoulders is 45 degrees to point of shoulder allowing for good reach. ***Shoulders***—Clean and narrow. ***Elbows***—Close to body. ***Legs***—Long, slender and straight. ***Pasterns***—Upright, fine and strong. Dewclaws may be removed. ***Feet***—Hare foot, narrow with elongated toes. Nails are trimmed to a moderate length.

Shoulders and elbows should not be so tight and narrow as to restrict movement, nor should they be floppy and loose. Legs should not be so slender as to appear breakable nor so long as to appear out of proportion. Legs should be long enough to dispel any idea of dwarfism, yet still retain the overall rectangular outline of the dog. Pasterns should have

Gangster of Love N'Co
winning Best of Winners
at the Sandemac Kennel
Club 1996 show.

*a very slight angle to give spring
to the step, the give that makes for
a smooth gait.*

Hindquarters—*Angulation*—
Stifle moderately angulated. From hock joint to ground
perpendicular. Dewclaws may be removed.

*The angulation of the hindquarters should be moderate
and complementary to the front angulation to give the dog
balanced movement and a smooth gait.*

Feet—Same as forequarters.

Feet are hare feet.

Coat—The Hairless variety has hair on certain portions of
the body: the head (called a crest), the tail (called a plume) and
the feet from the toes to the front of the pasterns and rear
hock joints (called socks). The texture of all hair is soft and

silky, flowing to any length. Placement of hair is not as important as overall type. Areas that have hair usually taper off slightly. Wherever the body is hairless, the skin is soft and smooth. Head Crest begins at the stop and tapers off between the base of the skull and the back of the neck. Hair on the ears and face is permitted on the Hairless and may be trimmed for neatness in both varieties.

Tail Plume is described under Tail.

The Powderpuff variety is completely covered with a double soft and silky coat. Close examination reveals long thin guard hairs over the short silky undercoat. The coat is straight, of moderate density and length. Excessively heavy, kinky or curly coat is to be penalized. Grooming is minimal—consisting of presenting a clean and neat appearance.

Hairless: Crest, plume and socks on the Hairless are single coat, soft and straight. The crest on the Hairless may be anything from a strip of hair from stop to neck to a full head of hair, complete with face furnishings and ear fringes.

Ch. Pandora's Ambrosia N'Co pictured winning Livingston Kennel Club's 1992 Winners Bitch award.

24

The crest of the Chinese Crested may vary. It can be anything from a strip of hair from the stop to the neck to a full head of hair. Socks may be just on the feet and sparse (in keeping with the crest) or heavy Clydesdale-type reaching up to about the pastern or hock joint. The tail plume matches the crest and socks in density and length. Hair may be left on the face and ears of the Hairless, or it may be trimmed from the face and ears of both varieties. A Hairless with a heavy crest and furnishings is more likely to have body hair. It may be a strip down the back or perhaps on the hips and shoulders. This does not make the dog a Powderpuff.

Powderpuff: The Powderpuff coat is a double coat with a soft, silky outercoat. Excess, be it in the amount of coat, kink or curl, is to be faulted. Sometimes humidity will bring out a wave in the coat; not all coats are absolutely straight. The coat should not be standoffish. Length is usually about knee-length or shorter. Coat length and density do vary in Powderpuffs. In some cases, due to the weight of the hair on the ears, they are trimmed.

Color—Any color or combination of colors.

The Crested is an interesting breed due to the infinite variety of colors and color combinations, plus the fact that

they change color and "tan" or darken in the sun. They also sunburn easily, particularly the light colors.

Gait—Lively, agile and smooth without being stilted or hackneyed. Comes and goes at a trot moving in a straight line.

The phrase "comes and goes...in a straight line" means simply no crabbing or sidewinding. The feet will come under the dog toward a point of balance, with legs in a straight line. The gait is smooth, not rolling.

Temperament—Gay and alert.

Cresteds are happy, people-loving dogs, especially with their own people. They are very versatile, trainable, attentive and anxious to please.

The Chinese Crested is an interesting breed due to the infinite variety of colors and color combinations.

RING PRESENTATION

Although not part of the standard or explanation of the standard, it is important to say a few words about ring presentation. Cresteds are presented in the ring much like any other toy dog. They are judged on the table, and they move rather fast. They need a bit of space to move out and show their ability to move correctly. In stacking a dog, whether or not to hold the tail up seems to be a major question. This depends on the dog and his natural tail carriage and set. If the dog carries it up, and especially if he holds it up a lot when standing, chances are it will be held up by the exhibitor. If not, it is allowed to drop. The Hairless may be shown with the tail down around the left hind leg to show the plume. Since the Hairless is naked, it gets cold and shivers and will tend to "ball up" to keep warm. Please keep environmental conditions, including protection from the sun, in mind when showing the Hairless.

Showing the Chinese Crested is much like showing any other Toy breed except that environmental conditions, including protection from the sun, should be kept in mind.

Even as I write this book and you read it, there is work afoot to change parts of the standard. I guess this process will continue as long as there are differences of opinions as to what is "winning" and what is considered "desirable."

ACQUIRING a Chinese Crested Dog

OWNING A PUREBRED DOG

So you've made the decision to expand your family by acquiring a dog. Remember, whatever the reasons for your decision, whether the dog is intended to be a companion or to compete in some aspect of the dog sport, it is important to take time in selecting the breed, variety, and bloodline, and to examine the environment the dog was raised in. Your new addition will be a member of the family for a long time. The Chinese Crested's life expectancy, for example, is 10 to 15 years.

Shop around and talk to different breeders. You can determine how reliable a breeder is by finding out how thoroughly he:

• Studies genetics, nutrition, structure and movement. A reliable breeder is concerned with producing puppies in an attempt to meet the ideal for the breed.

• Sees that all puppies receive appropriate inoculations according to their age and in consultation with a veterinarian.

• Is concerned with the humane treatment of all dogs and makes sure that his pups are placed with responsible owners in suitable homes.

• Takes personalized care with the raising and socialization of the puppies with other people and dogs in clean surroundings.

A litter of Chinese Crested puppies may be irresistible, but be certain to educate yourself about the responsibilities of owning a dog before you bring one home.

• Is in your area or nearby to assist you with the raising, feeding, training and grooming of your puppy, or at least will be willing to work with you closely by telephone.

• Will help you in your selection of a quality specimen to meet your needs and desires.

A reliable breeder should allow you to come visit with the puppy of your choice several times before you actually bring him home.

How do you find a reliable breeder? The American Kennel Club (AKC) can help. The AKC has two programs to assist in your endeavors.

Puppies should not leave their dam until at least eight weeks of age—it takes mom time to teach the facts of life. An 18-day-old litter with their Mom, "Mati."

1. The AKC Customer Service Department can supply you with educational information on acquiring a puppy, along with a geographical

listing of dog clubs. You can also receive the Breeders/Buyers Guide, which is a current listing of breeders advertising in the AKC's magazine, *Purebred Dogs/American Kennel Gazette*. Call (919) 233-9767 to receive your packet of information.

2. The AKC has a breeder referral program that will put you in contact with a breeder referral representative, who is a member of a local dog club, right in your own community. The referral program can be accessed for nominal cost by calling 1-900-407-PUPS (7877). After you specify the breed of dog you are looking for and your geographic area, you will be provided with the name and phone number of a breeder referral representative who works with dog clubs and breeders near you. The breeder referral representative will provide you with names of appropriate breeders near you and try to answer any questions you may have about the breed.

Puppies are very vulnerable when first born—they need lots of food, warmth and sleep.

MAKING THE DECISION

Once you have decided on the Chinese Crested and located a reliable breeder, you will be given entry to the special world of the Chinese Crested. Before you step over that threshold, I strongly urge you to have a written contractual agreement between you and the breeder. Have the contract spell out the price, conditions of ownership, breeding rights, stud rights, selection of stud service (if applicable), statement of quality of the dog, guarantees offered by the seller and conditions and explanation of return, refund or replacement of your purchase. Have the contract spell out how and when the obligations of both parties are considered fulfilled, and registration and/or transfer of ownership upon fulfillment of the contract.

A conscientious breeder will be concerned with preserving the quality of the breed and will always strive to produce the best puppies possible.

The days of the handshake are a thing of the past, but it's pretty hard to dispute what's in writing. Once the contract is signed, sealed and delivered—step over that threshold.

Be prepared to be the center of attention at dog shows, not to mention out in the general public, when the subject of your Crested arises. I have both varieties, Hairless and Powderpuffs. Often, the conversation, when the topic of dog shows comes up with members of the general public, resembles the following:

"What kind of dogs do you show?"

"Chinese Cresteds."

"What?"

"Chinese Cresteds."

"What do they look like? I don't think I've ever seen one."

"Well... if you took a Clydesdale horse and shrunk it down to about 11 to 13 inches high at the shoulders, you'll have the general appearance of the Hairless Chinese Crested. It's body is hairless with a (white, in my case) crest on the head and mane, (white) hair on its legs, like socks, and (white) hair on its tail called a plume. The Powderpuffs have the same structure but are covered with hair."

"Wow, do you have a picture of your dogs?"

"Why of course," I respond, as I proudly pull out a wallet full of my "win" pictures.

Even at dog shows, the most frequent question is, "What kind of dog is that?" The Chinese Crested is a unique and rather rare breed. It is estimated that there are over 9,900 AKC-registered Chinese Cresteds in the United States.

On April 15, 1994, I reluctantly agreed to drive to Oklahoma City to see one of these dogs. After some ten hours on the road, my wife and I pulled up in front of the breeder's home. The owner had three Hairless Cresteds out for a walk on leads. Before I even got out of the car I said, *"That's the one!"* My life as a Chinese Crested owner began with Mati, now Ch. Winsalot Maiden Chyna. At just eight months of age Mati finished her championship from the six- to nine-month puppy classes, with three five-point majors and three Bests of Breed at the Memorial Day 1994, weekend shows in Bloomington, Illinois. She attained her championship with a total of one four-point and three five-point major wins. Call it beginner's luck, but Mati has what it takes—she's my "dream come true."

BRINGING HOME THE CRESTED

You have chosen a lively, intelligent, devoted, affectionate, playful, sensitive, people-loving, versatile, anxious to please, extroverted and attentive little dog. I could think of a few more adjectives to describe the Crested, but I'm sure you get the message.

In general, there are two major differences physically between the Hairless and the Powderpuffs. The most obvious, of course, is the coat or lack of coat. The Hairless has a single

coat where hair is present, while the Powderpuff has a double coat. The double coat is

The only difference between the Powderpuff and the Hairless Chinese Crested, other than the coat, is the dentition. The Hairless may have missing teeth, crooked teeth or tusk-like canines.

You will find both hairless and coated dogs within the same litter of Chinese Cresteds.

comprised of thin guard hairs over the short silky undercoat. The other major difference is in the dentition. The Hairless may have missing teeth, crooked teeth or tusk-like canines. They may even be shaped differently. This is not a fault according to the standard. The Powderpuff should have a normal canine mouth and is faulted for missing teeth and a bad bite.

Normally as the permanent teeth grow in, the new ones weaken and push out the milk (puppy) teeth, making room for the permanent ones. I have noticed in several Crested puppies that they appear to have difficulty in readily losing their puppy teeth, especially the front ones. As a result the mouth may have two rows of teeth. If the milk teeth are not removed at the appropriate time, the dentition or the bite of the puppy may be ruined. This will cause the dog to be faulted according to the standard relating to teeth and bite.

It is important to have your vet look at the dentition and take corrective measures as needed. The preventive measures taken at the appropriate time will be extremely beneficial.

FEEDING Your Chinese Crested Dog

Nutrition is the science or study of properly balancing a diet to promote health. Dogs whose ages and activity levels differ have different nutritional requirements. The dog food market is flooded with a multitude of foods that claim to meet those various nutritional needs. There are foods for the active field-working dog, foods for the geriatric set and foods for puppies. Your personal feeding program should provide the very best nutritional meals for your dog depending on his stage in life.

My personal preference is to totally avoid any foods that have the words "by-products" in the ingredient list. The

Pick a high quality dog food that is nutritionally adequate and appropriate for your Chinese Crested.

Your Chinese Crested will feel very comfortable in his crate, and so it would not be out of the question to feed him there.

reason I make that choice is that "chicken by-products," for example, include such things as chicken beaks, feet and claws. Such chicken parts have little (if any) nutritional value. I also avoid canned dog food—not only because of the by-products but also because it is the most expensive dog food by volume.

I chose lamb and rice food as the optimal dog food after a conversation with a nutritionist. The lamb and rice combination continually proves to be the purest and most digestible food as compared to beef, liver, chicken and other standard dog food ingredients. When Mati, my first Crested, permitted me to be her family, I started her on lamb and rice kibble. Mati and the rest of our now expanded Crested family also get a vitamin treat every morning to ensure that they are getting all the nutrients they need.

I free-feed all my dogs, keeping food available to them at all times. No two dogs have the same appetite and eating habits. I adjust for the differences by watching the weight of the dogs. If I see one is underweight I'll supplement his food with a hamburger and rice combination (boiled hamburger and cooked rice in the broth with one cooked egg mixed in) or provide larger portions of the kibble in his or her crate when put away for a time. I have not had a problem with overweight dogs, but if I did I'd ration the food accordingly during feeding.

Fresh water is essential for all living creatures. Always have water available to your Chinese Crested whether indoors or out.

Good dental hygiene and nutrition go hand in hand. Tartar builds up whenever a dog is fed soft foods all the time. This build up of tartar is called gingivitis, which involves inflammation and subsequent infection of the gums. When gingivitis is present the gums appear swollen and red, and they

bleed easily. If allowed to continue unchecked, the build-up may have to be removed by the vet.

FEEDING THE BROOD BITCH

After breeding, I maintain the mother-to-be on the usual feeding routine for the first three to four weeks and supplement with a prenatal vitamin. These vitamins have additional calcium, vitamins and minerals. The mother will continue to need the prenatal vitamins until the puppies are weaned.

During the gestation period I watch the mother's weight. In the last three weeks of pregnancy, when she is larger, I feed her two or three smaller meals a day. This is to eliminate the uncomfortable feeling of one larger meal. I prepare the hamburger and rice recipe once a day with a little whole milk. The milk adds calcium and aids in the development of

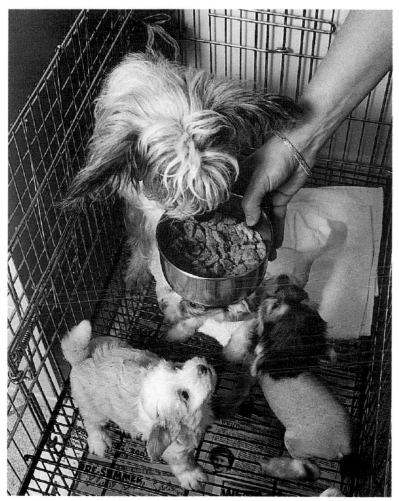

A nursing dam needs plenty of vitamins and extra nutrients while she nurses her pups. mother's milk for the puppies. Be careful, though, as too much whole milk can cause diarrhea.

Depending on the size of the bitch, I maintain the pregnancy diet for about a week after whelping. After that I continue feeding the same quantity, but cut down on the number of feedings. Then, keeping a watchful eye to make sure that the mother and puppies are progressing normally, I begin lessening the quantity as the puppies develop and begin to eat on their own.

Along with proper nutrition, part of the care of bitches in season is worming. There is very little controversy over the need to worm a bitch within a few days of the beginning of her season. Worming during pregnancy is more controversial. There are some schools of thought that say the bitch should be wormed 15 to 21 days after breeding. Others discontinue worming until the puppies are weaned. A lot depends on your veterinarian and possibly the use of caraside (for the prevention of heartworm).

PUPPY DIET

Growth and health of the puppies is directly based on nutrition received from the mother. If the mother has been properly taken care of, the puppies are likely to thrive. The first week is crucial, because they are exposed to the elements of the real world. They no longer are protected by the mother's womb. Under natural circumstances, the mother provides for their nutritional needs through nutrients and natural immunities contained in her milk.

On day three, have the veterinarian check the puppies for general health. You can have the dewclaws removed at this

POPpups™ from Nylabone® are 100% edible and enhanced with dog friendly ingredients like liver, cheese, spinach, chicken, carrots, or potatoes. They contain no salt, sugar, alcohol, plastic or preservatives. You can even microwave a POPpup™ to turn it into a huge crackly treat.

Carrots are rich in fiber, carbohydrates, and vitamin A. The Carrot-BONE™ by Nylabone® is a durable chew containing no plastics or artificial ingredients and it can be served to your Chinese Crested as is, in a bone-hard form, or microwaved to a biscuity consistency.

time. If you suspect that one of the puppies is not doing well, have the vet check for cleft palate. The puppy may not be able to suckle properly. You may have to feed the puppy yourself with an eye dropper containing a milk replacer.

When the puppies are about three weeks old, start feeding them a transitional cereal. This will provide a smooth transition from the mother's milk to solid foods. Give them the cereal in a supplemental or intermediate feeding. Thin it with a milk replacer to a consistency that the puppies can lap. Gradually increase the thickness as they learn to eat.

At week five or six, start to introduce and replace the cereal with soaked kibble, adding a little cottage cheese. As the puppies are weaned you may start them on solid puppy food. Use your judgment and common sense, making sure the puppies maintain good weight through a proper diet.

All puppies seem to be born with worms. Consider worming the pups as early as three weeks with a very mild wormer. Keep in mind, at any stage of growth, that all wormers are poison. Each time you worm, you could theoretically damage the dog's vital organs. It is therefore important not to worm the dog more than is necessary.

CARING for the Chinese Crested Dog

As a breed becomes popular and the number of litters increases, the obscure genetic traits become more noticeable. One such genetic problem that is becoming more prevalent in the Crested is Legg-Calve-Perthes Disease (LCPD). The exact etiology of LCPD in the dog is unknown, but it may be associated with abnormalities or inadequacy in blood supply to the thigh bone's rounded process, which was attached for a time to another bone by cartilage, but has become consolidated with the femur (thigh bone). The normal blood supply to the head of the thigh bone in adult dogs comes from three main sources. In puppies, however, there is only one blood supply to this rounded process: the interlacing blood vessels of the membrane surrounding the joint.

CAUSE AND EFFECT

A compromise of the blood supply to the rounded process that forms the head of the femur (thigh bone) leads to the death of the cells. The resulting changes in the bone structure can result in LCPD. Major symptoms are pain in the hip joint and disturbances of gait, usually of gradual onset and slow progression. Joint movements are limited, and the thigh muscles may become wasted. Several hypotheses have been used to explain the cause, namely: infection, trauma, genetic predisposition, metabolic and hormonal imbalances, as well as blood vessel abnormalities.

Your Chinese Crested will enjoy all the comforts of home—especially if he has his own bed to enjoy as well and a few Nylabone® products.

There is some experimental evidence that administration of male and female hormones in high doses can produce cellular changes in the rounded process of a puppy's thigh bone similar to early stages of LCPD.

A good breeder will raise litters only from parents that are free of genetic disorders.

The exact chemical or cellular changes that result in the structural changes have yet to be identified; however, reduction in blood supply due to either injury or some other non-infectious irritation has been proposed as the cause of the cellular death. Microscopic review of the rounded process that forms the head of the femur in dogs with naturally occurring LCPD reveals the presence of excessive growth of white connective tissue and accelerated activity of any one of the cells concerned in the formation of bony tissue relative to reparative activity. However, correction of the shape of the bony process does not occur. Severe and progressive degenerative arthritis (inflammation of the joint) is the resulting condition relative to LCPD.

X-Ray Examination

The appearance of x-rays of an affected hip joint will vary with the severity of the disease. The early changes are widening of the joint space, decreased density of the rounded protrusion constituting the head of the thigh bone and, frequently, hardening and thickening of the bone connecting the rounded protrusion with the thigh bone. As the disease progresses, the rounded protrusion takes on a moth-eaten appearance on x-ray. In the later stages, the shape of the head is completely lost and only a shriveled structure remains. Dogs in the advanced stage may show obvious fracture of the head and neck of the thigh bone on x-ray examination.

Prognosis and Treatment

Degenerative arthritis will result from LCPD in dogs. Approximately 25 percent of affected dogs recover from the lameness after several months of treatment. Non-surgical treatment consists of rest, limited exercise, well balanced nutrition and analgesic medications. Surgical treatment consists of removal of the head and neck of the thigh bone and the surgical reconstruction of a new and functioning joint (excision arthroplasty), that will successfully alleviate pain and signs of lameness in 85 to 95 percent of the animals, regardless of the stage of the disease. Thus, excision arthroplasty is the treatment of choice for LCPD in dogs.

SKIN—THE BARE NECESSITIES

The Hairless Chinese Crested has a unique set of problems that the Powderpuff does not. The Hairless is exposed to the elements and thus needs to have special care and consideration given to the "bare" facts. Let's start with an insight into some of the problems you may encounter.

The skin is the largest of the body's organs. It is supple, elastic tissue that conserves moisture and heat as well as provides information about the surroundings. Buried in the skin are millions of tiny nerve endings called receptors that sense touch, pressure, heat, cold and pain. Also embedded in the skin are many minute glands. There are sebaceous glands that produce a waxy substance to help keep the skin surface supple and perhaps prevent it from drying out.

There are thousands of hair follicles in the skin. These are pits of actively dividing cells that continuously make hairs. In addition, there are smaller hairs all over the body, some that can barely be seen by the unaided eye.

Skin is composed of two layers. The surface that you see is a thin covering called epidermis. Below the epidermis is a thicker layer, called the dermis. The dermis contains many specialized structures such as hair follicles. Below the dermis is a layer of fat that is called subcutaneous fat.

The surface skin layer, the epidermis, is a very active layer of cells. Cells at its base are continuously dividing to produce new cells, which gradually die as they fill up with a hard substance, keratin. As they die, they move up to the skin surface to be shed or worn away by rubbing action or washing.

In fact, virtually any movement that causes friction also causes some skin cells to be rubbed away. The continuous production of cells at the base of the epidermis keeps up with the continuous loss of cells from its surface. It takes an average of one month for any single epidermal cell to complete the journey from base to surface. On parts of the body where pressure and friction are the greatest, the epidermis is thicker, and the journey takes longer. A number of skin problems are caused by faults in the constant turnover of the skin cells.

Because the skin is on the outside of the body, you quickly notice any changes in appearance. There may be symptoms such as itching, swelling or, occasionally, pain. Diseases of the skin can be irritating and uncomfortable. In rare cases, serious diseases of the skin such as cancer or severe blistering can occur. However, most skin diseases only cause discomfort. That is not to minimize their effects because they can be quite bothersome.

The Hairless Chinese Crested needs special care and consideration given to his skin. Acne, the sun and the cold are a few of the problems he may face.

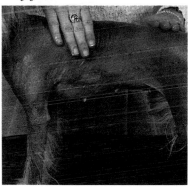

Acne Vulgaris

Acne vulgaris, often called simply acne, is a condition in which spots of various types appear on the skin. Acne is really a catch-all term for a variety of symptoms such as pimples, whiteheads and blackheads. It is a condition where the pores of the skin become clogged and inflamed lesions develop.

Almost every part of your dog is covered with hair, most of the hair virtually invisible. Each hair grows from a follicle, or tiny pit in the skin, and within each follicle is a sebaceous gland that produces an oily substance that lubricates the skin. If there is an over-production of oil and some of it becomes trapped in a follicle, bacteria can multiply in the blocked pit and cause it to become inflamed. The result is a pimple, which may be just a red lump or may become a pus-filled whitehead.

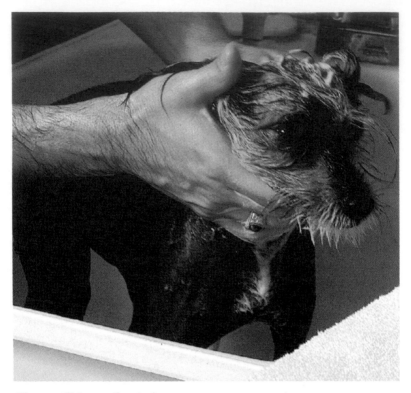

If your Chinese Crested suffers from overly oily skin you can apply a mixture of witch hazel and mouthwash to the skin every time you give the dog a bath.

Acne is a problem of adolescence; it nearly always develops during puberty (when sexual reproduction becomes possible) and usually clears up in later years. Acne occurs because the level of hormones in the body rises during puberty, and this stimulates the sebaceous glands to increase their production of an oily substance called sebum.

You can slow down the oil secretion by applying a homemade astringent directly to the skin. Apply a mixture of equal parts of witch hazel and mouthwash to the skin with cotton pads. Be careful about the areas around the eyes, mouth and other sensitive areas. The witch hazel acts as an astringent and the mouthwash has antiseptic properties. If the skin is very oily you can do this every time you bathe the dog.

Acne does not endanger general health. A follicle may become blocked, usually by a mixture of excess sebum and a dead skin cell, and a white plug forms over the pore or opening. The sebum, unable to escape, builds up in the blocked follicle. Bacteria normally present on the skin may infect the sebum, causing inflammation, pus and swelling that is an acne pimple.

What is the cause of all the clogging? Chocolate doesn't cause it (chocolate is poisonous to dogs). Sex, either too much or lack of it, doesn't cause it either. So what does? Heredity—at least for the most part. Acne is genetic; it is an inherited defect of the pores. If both the parents have acne, three out of four of the Hairless offspring will probably get it also.

Be careful of the product you use on your Chinese Crested. Many of those available on the market are too rich for his unique skin. Generally, those that are safe for puppies will be okay to use on your pet.

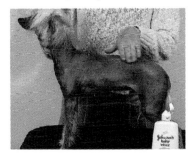

Oil-based lotions can exacerbate the problem. The pigments in lotions are not the problem, and neither is the water in the product. The culprit is just the oil. The oil is usually a derivative of fatty acids that are more potent than the dogs' own fatty acids. Use a non-oil-based product if your dog is prone to acne. Products that contain lanolin, isopropyl mysristate, sodium sulfate, laurenth-4 and D & C red dyes should be avoided. Like oil, these ingredients are too rich for the skin.

Here is an easy test that you can do at home to find out just how oily the products that you're using really are. Get a sheet of 25 percent cotton-bond typing paper and rub a thick streak of the product or lotion on it. Within 24 hours the oil will spread out and you will see a big grease ring—the more oil there is in the product, the bigger the grease ring. Stay away from products that produce large oil spots.

Remember—leave well enough alone. A pimple is an inflammation and you could add to the inflammation or cause an infection by squeezing it. Nothing can be done to a pimple to make it go away sooner. Normally a pimple will last from one to four weeks, but it will disappear eventually. A whitehead is a non-inflamed plugged core. The core of a whitehead is much smaller than the core of a blackhead. When you squeeze the whitehead, the wall of the pore could break and the contents could leak out into the skin and cause a pimple. A pimple naturally forms from the rupture of a whitehead pore wall. So I reiterate: No matter how great the temptation, you should never squeeze pimples or whiteheads.

The easiest way to avoid skin problems afflicting your Chinese Crested is to keep the skin clean. Bathing your dog on a regular basis will help.

Acne pimples may erupt on the nape of the neck, the back, the chest and the buttocks. If a pimple becomes more infected, it develops into a tender red lump with a white, pus-filled center. This tends to occur if you squeeze or pick at the eruptions, which is, unfortunately, a common reaction to unsightly areas of the skin. As individual acne pimples heal, others appear. Each healed pimple leaves behind a purplish mark, which usually fades away. Severely infected pimples may take many weeks to clear up and may leave noticeable scars.

Acne is classified in four grades, the first being a mild bout with a few whiteheads and blackheads. The fourth and most serious grade consists of many whiteheads, blackheads, pustules, nodules and cysts. Grade four acne is often accompanied by severe inflammation that becomes red or purple. It is also a sign that you should see your veterinarian. Severe acne may result in permanent scarring if it is not properly treated.

Self-Help—Above all, keep the skin clean. Wash it with an unscented soap daily, but not more often unless it becomes abnormally dirty or oily.

The coated Chinese Crested, or Powderpuff, will require extra care given to his coat. Grooming should be a part of your Crested's routine.

Sunshine helps in many cases of acne, but some acne medications may cause adverse reactions to sun exposure if your dog is being medicated. Therefore, minimize exposure to the sunlight, infrared heat lamps and sunscreens until you know how the skin will react. Do a patch test for sunscreen sensitivity. Finally, remember that picking and squeezing at pimples is likely to increase the problem.

If your dog has a mild case of acne, treating it yourself may help keep it under control. If it becomes severe, consult your veterinarian. Over-vigorous treatment of any kind is likely to do more harm to the skin than just leaving it alone.

You can fight back an acne attack with over-the-counter (OTC) products if you insist. OTC acne products come in various forms such as gels, liquids, lotion or creams. The water-based gel is recommended as it is less likely to irritate the Hairless's tender skin. Cleanse your dog's skin thoroughly before applying the product, and try using it for an hour or so in the evening. Then wash it off very thoroughly, especially around the eyes and neck, before putting your dog up for the night. OTCs

The hairless Chinese Crested must be protected against the sun's strong rays.

with benzoyl peroxide work well. The benzoyl pulls the peroxide into the pores and releases oxygen, which kills the bacteria that aggravates acne. It's like two drugs in one. The benzoyl also suppresses the fatty acid cells that irritate the pores.

Dry skin can be sensitive to benzoyl peroxide, so start with a lower strength product first, and increase the concentration slowly if needed. In most tests that have been conducted, the lower strength products were as effective as the stronger ones. Apply acne medication about half an inch around the affected areas to help keep the acne from spreading. The medication really doesn't fight pimples that are already there; you need to treat beyond the affected red inflammatory area.

Grooming and bathing your Chinese Crested are good ways to keep abreast of your dog's skin condition. Any change from the normal should be cause for concern.

Use one treatment at a time, don't mix treatments. If you arc using an OTC product, stop using it prior to using a prescription acne medication. Benzoyl peroxide is a close cousin to some prescription medications and other products containing vitamin A derivatives.

Professional Help—If the acne is severe enough to warrant professional help, your veterinarian will probably prescribe a special ointment that makes the skin peel and may also prevent new pimples from forming. If this treatment does not work, the veterinarian may prescribe small, regular doses of antibiotics for up to six months. If antibiotic treatment is unsuccessful or the acne is severe, your veterinarian may recommend treatment with drugs called retinoin. This is highly effective but may produce adverse side-effects. Retinoin should not be administered during pregnancy because it may cause fetal malformations.

THE SUN—GOOD AND BAD

Hairless Cresteds, although they do tan in the sun, are prone to sunburn. In the spring, the Hairless looks washed out because of the lack of a suntan. With a tan, the contrasting skin and furnishing colors give the Hairless an outstanding appearance. During the winter months I use a sun lamp to try and maintain the summer glow as long as I can, giving me a head start on the tanning process in the spring.

Pigmentation of the Hairless's skin can vary. The variation of pigmentation can cause different degrees of sunburn. Do not become careless. Use sunscreens to protect against the sun's burning rays. If by chance you accidentally do become careless, the following may be useful to you in helping to attain some degree of comfort for your beloved Crested.

Following a burn, the skin is inflamed. Cool it down with compresses dipped in any one of the following substances (if desired, you can direct a fan on the sunburned area to heighten cooling):

Cold Water—Use either plain water from the faucet or add a few ice cubes. Dip a cloth into the liquid and lay it over the burn. Repeat every few minutes as the cloth warms. Apply several times a day for a total of 10 to 15 minutes each.

Skim Milk—Milk protein is very soothing. Mix one cup of skim milk with four cups of water, then add a few ice cubes. Apply compresses for 15 to 20 minutes; repeat every two to four hours.

Aluminum acetate—If itching is intense, try mixing a powder containing aluminum acetate (available in pharmacies) with water. The aluminum acetate will keep the skin from getting too dry or itchy.

Oatmeal—Dermatologists recommend oatmeal water, which soothes the skin. Wrap dry oatmeal in a cheesecloth or gauze. Run cool water through it. Discard the oatmeal and soak the compresses in the liquid. Apply every two to four hours.

Witch hazel—Moisten a cloth with witch hazel and apply often for temporary relief. For smaller areas, dip cotton balls into the liquid and gently stroke on.

An alternative to compresses, especially for larger areas, is a cool bath. Add more liquid as needed to keep the water at the proper temperature. Afterwards, gently pat the skin dry with a clean towel. Do not rub the skin or you will irritate it further. The following substances can reduce pain, itching and inflammation:

Vinegar—Mix one cup of white vinegar into a tub of cool water.

Oatmeal powder—If the sunburn involves a large area, use the pre-measured packets or add one half cup of a prepared bath treatment made from oatmeal to a tub of cool water. Soak for 15 to 20 minutes.

Baking soda—Generously sprinkle baking soda into tepid bath water. Instead of toweling off, let the solution dry on the skin.

Soaks and compresses feel good and give temporary relief, but they can make the skin feel drier than before if you don't apply moisturizer immediately afterwards. Pat dry, then smooth on some bath oil. Let soak in for a minute, then apply a moisturizing cream or lotion. Some people use a topical cream that contains a little bit of cooling menthol.

Many of your natural household products, such as baking soda and oatmeal powder, can help keep your Crested's skin soft and luxurious.

You may wish to soothe skin irritation and inflammation with a topical lotion, spray or ointment containing 0.05 percent hydrocortisone. If there is an infection or if you are

worried that one will develop, you may want to use an over-the-counter antibacterial ointment.

If the burn is mild, an over-the-counter anesthetic can relieve pain and itching. Look for brands that contain benzocaine, benzyl alcohol, lidocaine or diphenhydramine hydrochloride. Aerosols are easier to apply than creams or ointments, but never spray them directly onto the face. Instead, put some on a piece of gauze or a cotton pad and dab it on the face, avoiding contact with the eyes.

Sleeping on a sunburn can be very uncomfortable, but a lot of rest is needed for the body to recover from the burn. Try sprinkling talcum powder on the bedding to minimize chafing and friction. It is a good idea to have plenty of fresh water available for your dog to help counteract the drying effect of a burn.

Be careful with blisters. Blisters indicate a fairly severe burn. If the blisters bother the dog and they cover only a small area, you may carefully drain them. But do not peel the top skin off—there will be less discomfort and danger of infection if air does not come into contact with the sensitive nerve endings.

Don't make the same mistake twice. After a bad sunburn, it takes three to six months for the skin to return to normal. When a sunburn is healing and the top layer of skin peels off, the newly exposed skin will be more sensitive than ever. That means your Hairless will burn even faster than before if you are not careful.

While the memory of the sunburn is still painfully fresh, brush up on your sun sense with these tips:

• Apply sunscreen about 30 minutes before exposing your dog to the sun, even if it is overcast. Harmful rays can penetrate cloud cover and, in fact, are often magnified by it. Don't forget to cover the entire dog with the sunscreen.

• Take extra care between the hours of

Apply a sunscreen to your Chinese Crested's skin every time you go outdoors. Even when the temperature is cold, your Crested is still susceptible to sunburn if the sun is out.

10:00 A.M. and 3:00 P.M. (11:00 A.M. and 4:00 P.M. daylight saving time), when the sun is at its hottest.

CLIMATIC AND GEOGRAPHIC DIFFERENCES

North, south, east or west, climate varies, but common sense is the primary element in the care you give your Crested. I have found that Powderpuffs are more tolerant of colder temperatures, most likely because of their coats. Conversely, Hairless are more tolerant of the warmer climate. However, both Puffs and Hairless thrive in all climates and temperatures if you use common sense.

You can allow your Crested to slowly get a tan by exposing him to the sun's rays a little at a time.

Here in the Midwest, I allow the Hairless to slowly get a suntan in early spring by exposing them to the rays a little at a time, much like you would your child. However, if you obtain your Hairless in mid-summer and he has not tanned well, use an oil-free sunscreen until he acquires a suntan. A moisturizer should be used so the skin doesn't dry out.

The Hairless have sweat glands while the Puffs do not. That is nature's cooling system, but the first consideration for both varieties, especially in a climate with dry heat, must be to provide plenty of fresh water and ample shade when they are let out to play and exercise. Be extremely careful of sunburn and dehydration. The Puffs have a slightly different problem; for instance, a black dog's coat will have a tendency to change to a reddish cast after over-exposure to the sun. So if you are striving to keep a beautiful black coat, think twice about the length of time the dog is exposed to the sun.

In the colder months and colder regions, the key words about protection from the elements are common sense. The Puffs and the Hairless are not equipped to cope with the cold as are some other breeds, such as Huskies. Some people say that the Crested will acclimate to the colder temperatures. Let me ask you a question: How long would you be willing (or able) to stay outside in your swimsuit in temperatures of 30,

40, 50 or even 60 degrees? How then can you expect a Hairless to stay out even longer with less on? Remember—the dog's normal body temperature is 102 degrees, which is higher than ours, so proportionately it is even colder for the dog than it is for you. The Puffs can stand the colder temperature a little longer than the Hairless because of their coats. It is very important to help the Hairless with some man-made protection such as a sweater or the like. After all, you dress appropriately for the weather, and you must help the Crested do the same.

HAIRLESS AND THE WIND CHILL FACTOR

Frostbite

Frostbite occurs when the skin and underlying body tissues freeze. The body shuts down circulation to the extremities in an effort to preserve core heat. This makes it possible for dogs (particularly the Hairless) to be severely affected whenever there are below freezing temperatures, high winds (wind chill) or dampness. The flow of the blood to the affected area stops and in severe cases skin cells may be permanently damaged. Any part of the body can be affected but feet, noses and ears are most at risk. Frostbitten skin is hard, pale and cold, and the animal no longer has feeling in it.

Your Chinese Crested is unable to tell you that he is overheated or that he is cold, so be sure to always check his temperature.

Frostbite develops in three stages. The first indication is a reddening of the skin. In the second stage, blisters form on the affected area. The final stage involves death of skin cells and underlying tissue. As the frostbitten area thaws, the skin becomes reddish and painful.

Your Hairless Chinese Crested must be protected from the colder weather as well as from the sun. In the cool of springtime a lightweight coat should suffice to keep your Crested warm.

Treatment: *Medical myth*—The best way to deal with frostbite is to rub the affected area with snow. *Wrong!* This approach causes further damage because of the friction with the skin and the additional loss of heat from dampness. *Reality*—A steady, fast re-warming is the right treatment. Get the dog inside as soon as possible. If you can't get inside, shelter the dog from the wind, give him warm drinks and either cover the frozen body parts with a blanket or warm the dog against your body. *Do not* use radiant heat, such as a heat lamp, and *never* rub the affected areas. Frostbite must be treated promptly. Every minute of delay lessens the chances of recovery. Memorize the instructions for dealing with this problem, especially if you will be in a place where professional medical help may not be readily available.

Puppies have a lower body temperature than adults. Extra attention must be paid to keeping the puppies warm during the colder weather. These two pups seem content in their nice warm bed.

Hypothermia

A grown dog's body temperature range is normally 101–103 degrees Fahrenheit, and lower in puppies. During prolonged exposure to the cold, more body heat may be lost than can be replenished, so the body temperature may drop. This is known as hypothermia. Even a 6 degree drop—barely noticeable in air temperature—could be enough to kill a human.

In young healthy dogs, hypothermia may occur after prolonged physical exertion in cold windy conditions. As the dog depletes his stores of energy, body temperature falls, causing a gradual physical slowing that may pass unnoticed. The dog becomes increasingly clumsy, irritable and sleepy, and begins to shiver uncontrollably. There may be confusion, drowsiness and eventually coma, with slow weak breathing and heart rate. This condition requires immediate medical attention. Elderly dogs and very young puppies are affected even more easily.

Prevention

For both frostbite and hypothermia, prevention is the best treatment. Use common sense and be careful whenever you

Always use common sense whenever you expose your Chinese Crested to inclement weather.

expose your dog to inclement weather conditions. Bear in mind that the Hairless do not have the natural protection most dogs have. They are as vulnerable as you would be if you went outside without wearing any clothes. In fact, the metabolism of the Hairless is higher than that of other dogs and therefore their energy stores are depleted more quickly, causing both frostbite and hypothermia to occur more rapidly. Keep in mind that a dog—or for that matter a person—can suffer from hypothermia even if inside a shelter. It is important to maintain the body temperature at normal levels.

Temperature and the Wind Chill

When banks and billboards flash the time and temperature they usually show it first in Celsius (C) and then in Fahrenheit (F). To help you understand the relationship between the two, the following conversion formulas are useful.

When dressing your Chinese Crested for the outdoors, take into cosideration what the wind chill factor is and dress your dog accordingly.

Changing Celsius to Fahrenheit:

F = 9/5 x C + 32

Example: Celsius = 30 Degrees

F = (9/5 x 30) + 32

= (9 x 30)/5 + 32

= (270/5) + 32

= 54 + 32 = **86 degrees F**

Changing Fahrenheit to Celsius:

C = 5/9 x (F - 32)

Example: Fahrenheit = 86 degrees

C = 5/9 x (86 - 32)

= 5/9 x 54

= (5 x 54)/9

= 270/9 = **30 degrees C**

Weather reports on television, radio and newspapers during the winter months will add the wind chill index to their reports. This is also sometimes called the comfort index, and was developed to describe mathematically what the affects on the body are when the temperature is further decreased because of the wind.

If you are standing outside in 0°F temperatures with no wind, it feels like 0°F. If, however, the wind is blowing 15 m.p.h., it feels like -31°. Wind chill factors of -10° to -20° below zero are considered bitter cold. When the factors register lower than -20°, it is considered extremely cold. In extreme cold unprotected flesh will begin to freeze in about one minute. Keep this in mind when you let your Crested out for a run. Make it a short run and put a coat or sweater on your Hairless.

When grooming or bathing your Chinese Crested, take the opportunity to check him for any abnormalities.

CHECK-UP FOR PREVENTION

When grooming or bathing your dog, you can do double duty by checking for irregularities at the same time. This is an important routine that should be established. The inspection will only take a few minutes now but could save you a lot of time and money later, not to mention prevent problems for your dog. Avoiding problems and detecting warning signs as early as possible will lead to a healthier and happier dog.

Dogs can't tell you what is ailing them, but their bodies can give you clues as to their general health. Get into the habit of routinely checking as you are grooming and bathing your little one(s).

1. **Skin**—You have taken the time to bathe your Crested and have taken special care with the skin. When either the Hairless or Powderpuff is wet, check for red or raw areas and for signs of infection due to allergies or abrasions.

2. **Mouth**—Inspect the lip area for any irregularities. Look inside the mouth, inside the lips and under the tongue, checking for inflamed gums, excess tartar, pale gums and other abnormalities.

3. **Ears**—Smell and check the ears for mites. These could cause problems if not handled promptly.

4. **Nose**—Check the nose for loss of pigmentation. It could be genetic, medical or simply a need for a different material for the food bowl.

Inspecting the mouth is as important as inspecting the rest of your Chinese Crested. Inspect the lip areas, inside the mouth, inside the lips and under the tongue.

5. **Eyes**—Look for redness in the whites of the eyes. Check for clarity. Look at the eyelids for small growths or inflammation. An allergy can cause excess tearing.

6. **Paws**—While checking the paws, check the base of the nails for inflammation, fungus and redness. Look for cuts, punctures or bruises on the pads. Trim the hair between the pads even with the pads. If the dog has been licking his paws, there may be a rust-colored stain. This could indicate a cardiovascular problem. It is good to trim the dog's nails after the bath while they are still soft.

7. **Hindquarters**—Learn how to empty the anal glands. When emptying the glands, a brown secretion is normal. Any other color could indicate an infection. Small rice-like grains or balls in the stool or anal area are a sure sign of tapeworms. Tapeworms could cause coat coarseness on your dog.

8. **Coat**—While checking the coat, look for areas that may have been chewed. Make sure there are no mats between the toes, as these could cause an infection and discomfort for the dog.

9. **Irregularities**—When drying and grooming the dog, carefully feel with your fingertips to locate any irregularities, such as lumps, tumors and/or cysts. Be especially careful with the hairbrush and comb around any areas in which you find an irregularity. This is a good time to weigh the dog. Is there a loss or gain?

10. **Overall**—General appearance and impression can give you a feel for the dog's general health. Is he lethargic or sluggish? Does he seem alert?

Take care of your dog—you will be rewarded with unparalleled, undying and unconditional love and devotion.

BREEDING Your Chinese Crested Dog

Before deciding to breed your Chinese Crested, ask yourself, "What am I trying to accomplish by breeding?" From my perspective, when you have chosen to breed the Crested, or any other dog for that matter, you have taken on the responsibility of preserving and enhancing the essential qualities, physical characteristics and attributes of that breed. If you are not prepared to do this, don't breed. If you are thinking that there is a lot of money to be made, you are in for a rude awakening.

Let's assume that you have all the good intentions of a responsible breeder. First you must study the breed standard and know it thoroughly. You must know the desirable characteristics as well as the undesirable ones, and breed for improvement rather than just for cute puppies. They don't stay puppies for long.

A good breeder is an individual who looks at and breeds the dogs with a holistic eye; individuals who can admit to weaknesses and faults in their own dogs and not just those belonging to others. Further, a good breeder should be able to accept constructive criticism, not be a thin-skinned individual with tunnel-vision. There is yet to be a perfect dog created. When there is, the standards will change. Study the pedigrees of the bloodlines you are interested in breeding into and compare them with yours for compatibility and breed improvement. Pedigrees may be used to determine the lineage

A newborn litter of Chinese Cresteds is shown here with a lighter included to give a scale as to how small these creatures are.

of potential studs or bitches. However, just because a dog has Ch. (champion) in front of its name does not alone ensure quality. Some dogs have become champions with stiff competition and some because of the lack of good competition. Keep in mind that the lack of a champion title does not necessarily mean the animal is of poor quality. It may be because of lack of exposure. If at all possible, try to see as many dogs in the

Responsible breeders ensure that good health and temperament are passed down to each generation.

The antibodies in their mother's milk will protect the pups from disease until they are old enough to be vaccinated.

pedigree as you can and evaluate them yourself. Look for qualities that have

endured from generation to generation and see how genetics has affected the lineage.

GENETICS

The study of genetics is an extensive field; however, knowledge of genetics does not guarantee a successful breeding program. To date there has been little research on the genetics of dogs. In fact, much of what is known is in the more uncomplicated areas such as color, eye defects, coat texture, coat color, etc. The breeding of dogs is more of an art than an exact science. As this book is designed for the new owner of the Chinese Crested, I'll give an overview of genetics as it relates to the Crested.

Dogs have 39 pairs of chromosomes, each containing 25,000 genes. This alone makes the genetic possibilities almost limitless. One gene is inherited from each parent. When two genes are different, one would be dominant and the other recessive. The dominant gene is expressed and the recessive gene is suppressed, but the recessive trait could appear in later generations when two recessive genes come together. Many undesirable hereditary traits are expressed by recessive genes, which can be carried down through many generations. An inherited trait may be the result of the action of more than one pair of genes and of some gene pairs both expressing themselves.

We can determine the ratio of both genotype and phenotype expected from a given genetic cross. The term genotype refers to the type of genes in an individual and phenotype to the expression of the genes. For instance, a person with genotype of (Aa) or (AA) would have a phenotype of normal pigmentation (nonalbinisim), whereas an individual with genotype (aa) will have the phenotype of albinism.

We need terms to differentiate between individuals who carry two dominant genes for a particular trait and those who carry one dominant and one recessive. If the trait is fully dominant, the individuals will look alike, at least for that trait, but their offspring can be quite different. Those with two genes alike are called homozygous for that pair of genes, while those who have one gene of each kind are called heterozygous.

We know there are two types of Crested: the Hairless and the Powderpuff. The two varieties are inseparable because of their genetic make-up. Hairlessness in dogs is the result of an incomplete dominant mutation, which is lethal when homozygous. Every Hairless Crested carries the dominant gene for hairlessness (Hr) and the gene for a normal coat (hr). Every Hairless carries a lethal gene, as (Hr) is dominant over the recessive (hr). Thus the Hairless is referred to as (Hrhr).

When and why are these genes lethal? Some genes so alter the phenotype as to lower the chances of survival. Some genes may interfere and cause death shortly after fertilization. Others may prevent survival of the embryo when it is a microscopic ball of cells. Still others may not take effect until the embryo is fully formed. Many cause death shortly after birth because they prevent the normal functioning of the lungs, kidneys or heart.

At six-and-a-half weeks old, this litter of Chinese Crested pups is resting comfortably. Note that there is one Hairless in this litter of Powderpuffs.

The Powderpuff does not carry the hairless (Hr) gene, only the gene for coat (hr), thus the Powderpuff is referred to as (hrhr). This combination is not lethal.

Pity the poor puppy that gets a double dose of the hairless gene (HrHr), for he shall not survive, while those with a single dose of (Hr) will survive. On the other hand, a puppy may get a double dose of (hrhr), resulting in a Powderpuff.

The mating of two Hairless (Hrhr) x (Hrhr) would result in the following average combinations, assuming a litter of four:

1 (HrHr) Homozygous Hairless—Death, lethal genes
2 (Hrhr) Heterozygous Hairless—Will survive
1 (hrhr) Homozygous Powderpuff—Will survive

Mating a Hairless (Hrhr) to a Powderpuff (hrhr) would net the following average results:

2 (Hrhr) Heterozygous Hairless—Will survive
2 (hrhr) Homozygous Powderpuffs—Will survive

Unfortunately, nature is not that predictable. The first two mentioned matings, combining two Hairless or a Hairless to a Powderpuff, could produce all Hairless or all Powderpuffs.

The final combination of Powderpuff (hrhr) to a Powderpuff (hrhr) will have the result of:

4 (hrhr) Homozygous Powderpuffs—Will survive

Please note that none of the Powderpuffs will carry the hairless or lethal genes.

The degree of hairlessness in the Hairless is unpredictable. The hairlessness could range from sparse to dense on the body where the hair is unwanted. To confirm a hairy Hairless as a true Hairless, check the dentition. If the canines are tusk-like (pointed forward), the dog is a Hairless. The Powderpuff will have normal dentition.

Good luck on your breeding program, but don't make any bets as to what the litter is going to produce, unless you breed two Powderpuffs.

WHELPING

Gestation period is near its end. The puppies are due any day or hour. You have been relentless in maintaining a good feeding program. Your anxiety and enthusiasm for the moment increases with every whimper from your little mother-to-be.

You are prepared. You've read all the books available on the subject of whelping. You may even have one or two close at hand for quick reference. You have your veterinarian's phone number handy in case of an emergency. All of the equipment and supplies are neatly laid out on a surface near the whelping pen.

However, with the Crested you may encounter a minor problem that was not addressed in some of the books that you've read. Cresteds are considered free whelpers, so you should not encounter any unusual conditions other than those that can occur with any breed. The only uncommon problem you may encounter is the Hairless bitch's inability to bite

Breeding a litter of puppies does not end with the birth. Socialization and vaccinations, as well as a lot of love, are all part of the breeding process.

Six-and-a-half-week old litter nursing from their mother, "Mati." Pups will continue to nurse from their mother until their puppy teeth become too uncomfortable for her to bear, usually at eight to ten weeks of age.

through the umbilical cord, which may be due to the dog's unusual dentition. She may not have any teeth at all or her teeth may be wide-spread. In this case, you should be prepared to assist in severing and tying off the cord. You will probably not have the same problem with a Powderpuff bitch with good dentition.

Whether Hairless or Powderpuff, I like to wrap the tail with self-adhesive cloth gauze. I do this to prevent having one of those long hairs entangle the puppy and possibly strangle it. It is also a lot easier to maintain cleanliness during whelping. I also like to make sure the underside hair is removed so the puppies can easily access the mother for feeding. If you don't want to clip the hair off the hindquarters, try wrapping the legs with the self-adhesive gauze as well.

You may also want to consider cutting the leg portion off of a white cotton sweat sock for use as a snood to keep the hair on the crest, ears and neck from getting soiled during whelping. Simply slide an open end over the head and ears down to the neck.

It is extremely important to maintain a warm environment for the puppies. The puppies should not be exposed to cold drafts or low temperatures. Immediately after they are born, dry the puppies carefully. Although the Powderpuffs are born with hair, there is no difference in the protection from the elements they need compared to that required by the Hairless.

Consistency of type and reliable temperament, along with good health and soundness, are the goals of all responsible breeding programs. Improving the breed and producing healthy, typey Cresteds must be strived for with every litter.

Make sure you account for all the placentas during the whelping. I know of a breeder who almost lost an entire litter and the mother because one was retained. In a matter of 24 hours the retained placenta poisoned the mother's entire system including the milk, which was passed on to the puppies. The breeder did lose two of the litter. The rest had to be bottle-fed almost from the time they were born, and with special medication and formulas this is a long, arduous and expensive process.

You should remove each newborn to a warm holding area while the mother is delivering another brother or sister. A cardboard box lined with towels works well. Under the box I place a heating pad with thermostatic controls to maintain a desired temperature. After the latest newborn is dried and the mother has done nature's thing, I re-unite the puppies with their mother. She is far better for comfort and correct temperature than anything human beings can contrive.

I keep a record of the time each puppy is born, its weight and a description of the puppy. You'll be surprised how quickly they will change in weight and color.

When the puppies are ready to come, make sure you're ready for them. Be well prepared (and well rested, as you never know what time it will happen!) for the big event.

Many breeders keep very accurate records on every birth, including the time each puppy was born, its weekly weight and a description of the puppy.

TRAINING Your Chinese Crested Dog

There are three basic things to remember when training your puppies. First, make it a fun experience. Second, don't overdo each training session. Short periods of five minutes, three times a day, are far better than one 15-minute session. Third, praise and reward, praise and reward, more praise and reward. You'll find that following these basics will yield untold benefits later in both the show ring and everyday life at home.

A good show dog needs to have a certain winning attitude, one that shows confidence and competitiveness—a sparkle that says, "I'm a winner." It is good training that gives a dog these attributes. This type of positive training program begins at birth. It is never too early to start developing and enhancing desirable traits, so even before the eyes and ears are open you should hold, stroke and pet the puppies several times a day to get them accustomed to being handled. As pups develop and grow, you'll notice that each has a personality of its own. One may be more aggressive, curious and obviously dominant, while the others are more laid-back. Start evaluating their personalities at birth and watch their progress. It will give you an idea of what personality areas each pup will need work on.

Prior to outside socialization, I use a desensitization audio tape. The tape has a variety of sounds such as crowd noises, auto horns, accidents, sirens, fireworks, thunder storms and more. I start playing the tape at a very low volume and increase it over an extended period of time until it is at a realistic level. I

Basic obedience training is a must for your new Chinese Crested; it does not just teach him acceptable behavior, it keeps him safe as well.

don't want the puppies' first experience of these sounds to be their first time outside. Encountering many new stimuli at once could be traumatic for them. There will be enough other noises and distractions for them to cope with on their outings. During the desensitization efforts, I also introduce the puppies to lead breaking, socialization, the grooming and presentation table, stacking/presentation and showing their teeth and bite.

Encountering too many new stimuli at once could be traumatic for your Chinese Crested puppy. Slowly introduce him to the new sights and sounds he will be experiencing.

Outside socialization must begin when your Chinese Crested is still a puppy. Your pup should be slowly desensitized to the noises that it will encounter while outdoors.

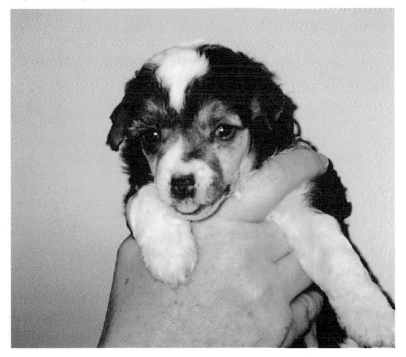

LEAD BREAKING

Your puppy should be taught to walk freely on a leash and have good manners, especially if you are planning to show. No judge is amused by a dog that is untrained and cuts capers in the show ring. At a "puppy fun match" this behavior may be acceptable, but not when competing for championship points.

Walking on lead is one of the most important lessons you will teach your Chinese Crested.

Start by placing a small collar on the puppy so he gets used to having something around his neck. When the puppy has been acclimated to the collar, replace it with a lead and let him drag it for about five minutes or so. Stay with the puppy during this time to make sure the lead doesn't get tangled and injure the dog. It is best to do this three or four times a day. Occasionally hold the lead to put a slight tension on it, thereby introducing another sensation. When the pup becomes accustomed to the feel of having the lead held, encourage him to come to you with a slight tug. Enticing the pup with a treat is very strong motivation for him to listen. Once the puppy is comfortable with this action and moves about freely on the lead with you, it is time to expose the little one to the outside world.

Never try to lead or drag the puppy away from the house or familiar territory. Carry the pup about 50 feet or so away from the house, constantly talking to and comforting him. Put the puppy on the ground and then lead, praise and treat him back to the house several times a day. The next step will be to start walking to and from the house in several different directions. Accustom your puppy to walking on your left side and to moving out smartly and staying abreast, neither lunging nor lagging, while you praise, treat and pet. Let your dog lead you for the first few minutes so that he fully understands that freedom can be his if he goes about it properly. If while walking he starts pulling in one direction, all you do is stop walking. He will walk a few steps and then find that he can't walk any further. He will probably turn and look you in the eye. This is the critical point of the training. Just stand right there and stare back at him. Then, walk about ten feet and stop again. As before he'll walk to the end of the lead, find he can't go any further and turn around and look at you. If he starts to

pull, jerk and jump around, just stand there again. After he quiets down, bend down, comfort him, praise him and give him a treat, as he may be frightened. Keep up this training until he learns not to outwalk you and to behave properly. Make it a happy and fun experience.

SOCIALIZATION

Most breeders feel that the critical period of any puppy's life, in regard to the development of temperament through socialization, to be the period between the ages of 21 days and four months. Puppies raised under kennel conditions with little human contact up to five weeks of age will tend to show fear reactions later in life. However, if they are handled by humans after five weeks of age, this shy tendency can be averted. If they are not handled until they are 12 weeks of age, and they are timid and shy, it will be much more difficult to re-train them. After 21 days of age, the

Accustoming your Chinese Crested to being handled from puppyhood will make grooming and other similar tasks easier when he is an adult.

Puppies that are removed from their litter and given brief daily periods of individual attention learn to adapt more easily to humans.

puppy starts to learn and needs daily periods of socialization with humans. When a puppy is removed from the litter for brief daily periods and given individual attention and mild discipline, he will learn more easily to adapt to humans. When he finally leaves his litter for good, he will accept his new owners more readily and respond easily to most of his new owner's wishes and environment.

A critical age is five to six weeks, and thereafter when the puppy goes to his new home. This is a traumatic change, and it should be as gentle a transition as possible. An unhappy puppyhood can leave a marked impression on the pup's temperament for the rest his life. It is strongly suggested and urged not to separate littermates into new homes until they are at least a minimum of eight weeks old, and 12 weeks is even better, as they will be better prepared and adjusted for the transition.

It is also strongly suggested not to take puppies out in public until they have had all of their inoculations. Once that hurdle is cleared, however, introduction to the public is essential. This is an additional part of socialization training. Take the pups to a strip mall and walk back and forth in front of the stores. This is the time to introduce the pup to strangers, but never force the puppy to do anything. If necessary, pick up the puppy and let people pet him. Puppies must get accustomed to strangers, as they will encounter crowds of nothing but strangers at dog shows. What you want is a well-adjusted dog.

Some pet store owners encourage you to bring your dogs into their establishments. Walking up and down the aisles amid other animals and distractions is an excellent training experience. Some, if not all, all-breed dog clubs offer conformation training classes. These classes simulate what happens in the show ring. Take advantage of this type of class to benefit your dog's training and to learn or brush up on your own ring skills. This will help the two of you to establish the routine you'll use if you decide to pursue a show career. Your aim in all these activities is to develop a confident and well-adjusted puppy.

GROOMING AND PRESENTATION TABLE

For proper perspective and ease of evaluation, smaller breeds such as the Crested are presented on a table for examination by the show judge. It is therefore essential for the puppy to be confident while on the table. To develop that poise, I place the dog on the table and let him roam about and explore the new territory—guarding, of course, against mishaps such as falling off. Once the puppy gets accustomed to this experience, I introduce the grooming and stacking aspects of the training.

At very early stages of training it is important not to confuse the dog with mixed experiences about a piece of equipment, particularly the table. In most cases, the grooming table and presentation table are approximately the same size and height. You need to separate the two experiences to eliminate possible confusion. The grooming table is where all the not-so-fun things happen, such as nail clipping, combing, drying, trimming, detangling, so on. The stacking table, on the other hand, is where the dog must be at his best, so it should be associated with happy, enjoyable experiences.

Most people have one table for both grooming and practice stacking (presenting). Even if this is your situation, you can easily separate the experiences. When using the table to practice stacking, place a different piece of material, such as a piece of plywood, on the table top. This gives a different feeling on the dogs' paws. Better yet, move the table out of the grooming area so the dog is disassociated from the grooming experience before practicing stacking. The best situation is to have two tables, one for grooming and one for stacking.

STACKING AND PRESENTATION

Before you can stack and present the dog, you must know what a picture-perfect presentation looks like. You need several points of reference. You need to know the structure of your dog compared to the AKC standard and how other experienced handlers show a dog. To obtain this, evaluate your dog objectively by comparing him to the standard. Take note of both his good and bad points, avoiding tunnel vision. Then go to dog shows and watch how Cresteds are presented by experienced handlers. Don't be

In order to stack and present your Chinese Crested properly, you must know the structure of your dog compared to the AKC standard, and be able to show off his best points.

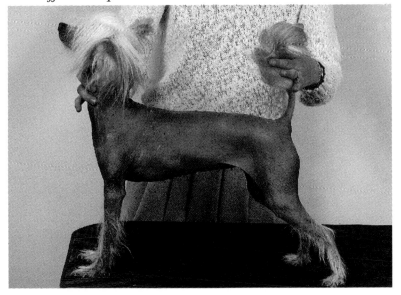

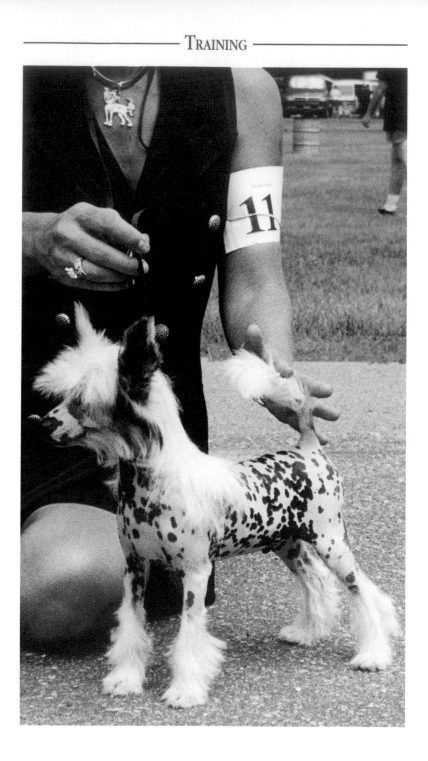

afraid to ask questions, most people are willing and eager to help the novice. After all, it is one of their favorite topics and it gives them a chance to promote the breed.

Strive to create a picture in which your dog is perfectly stacked in accordance with the standard, is properly groomed, and has a positive attitude. A still camera and a video camera are extremely helpful in assessing your presentation. They also provide an excellent record of your progress.

When stacking and showing your dog, all aspects of the breed's standard should be kept in mind.

The easiest way to stack a dog is to first position the front paws correctly. The front legs should be directly under the shoulders with the paws very near the front edge of the table. Then place the rear legs so the hocks are perpendicular to the table. Talk to the dog constantly, assuring him that everything is okay. Once the legs are in proper position, stroke the topline (back) to make sure it is level, not roached (arched). If the topline is sagging, a gentle prod in the stomach area will straighten it. All of this should be done in ten seconds. You need to be ready and waiting for the judge, not have the judge waiting for you.

With a mental picture of how your dog should look while stacked on the table, start practicing your stacking routine. Attempt to stack the dog in ten seconds. You should avoid having the stacked dog look like a rocking horse in profile, meaning that the dog is posted (front legs out in front of the dog instead of under the shoulders) and rear legs are stretched out so far behind the dog that he lacks stability. A good way to check out the posture is to stack the dog in front of a mirror.

After you think you have the dog stacked properly, have someone take a picture of him in the stacked position. Study *Stacking and presenting your Chinese Crested properly takes a lot of practice. Ch. Stop Badgering Me N'Co is being shown off nicely by his handler.* the pictures, pick out the faults and practice correcting them. Look at the pictures through the eyes of a judge and critique them.

Stopping your dog in front of the judge is another critical part of presentation. Your Chinese Crested and you should practice stopping in a position that is reflective of the picture-perfect stack.

Now start moving the dog as you would at a dog show. This is where the video camera becomes invaluable. Pictures don't lie and are very helpful. Your main objective here will be to determine the proper speed to move your dog. The gait should look natural, neither fast and forced nor slow and lazy, but purposeful. Try to match the speed that the dog uses when he is interested in something and moves toward it with poise and confidence (but not running). Practice at different speeds while you are being filmed. Pick out and practice the speed that best replicates the speed and look of the natural gait.

When moving the dog, try to keep the lead loose. This will allow the dog to move naturally; all you have to do is keep up with him. Using a tight (taut) lead will restrict the dog's movement, causing him to move unnaturally and ruin the presentation.

In the show ring you are required to stop in front of the judge after each movement you are asked to perform. The judge will then assess the dog in his natural stance. You need to practice stopping, endeavoring to get the dog to stop in a position reflective of that picture-perfect stack. This is another critical part of presentation.

Your clothing is another facet to be considered in presentation. Your attire needs to be in good taste and complimentary to the color of your dog. You want your dog to stand out rather than blend into nothingness. I would suggest wearing something that smoothly contrasts with the dog. Don't wear a black outfit if your dog

During shows, trips or other long-term outings, always bring your Crested's crate so that he may have a safe place to retreat to when needed.

is black or a white outfit if your dog is white. Choose your outfits with as much thought as you did when you chose your Crested— carefully.

CRATE TRAINING

Obviously, dogs can't be allowed to roam freely about the home. The dog crate is the logical solution. Crates arc uscd to transport dogs to and from dog shows, the vet's office, etc. They are durable and are accepted by the airlines for shipping. Crates offer several other advantages in addition to shipping and transporting. They also aid in housebreaking the puppies and give the dogs a safe haven, a place of security and ownership. Crates afford owners the ability to separate their dogs if necessary. Crates help in preventing accidents and aid in recuperation, as well as in protection from the elements.

When you go to a dog show, you'll see crates of all sizes and materials, from plastics to metals. It is an accepted and expected practice to crate dogs at dog shows. It is no more cruel than putting an infant child in a crib or an enclosed playpen for their safety and security.

Crate training can start before the puppies are weaned as they start moving around and exploring their surroundings.

The ideal crate size for the grown Crested measures 27"L x 20" W x 19" H. This is large enough to allow the dog to stand up, turn around and lie down. It is also small enough to assist in housebreaking. Dogs don't like to soil where they have to sleep.

Before the puppies are weaned, place the crate in a position that will allow access to it from the whelping pen. This will permit the mother to separate herself from the puppies for periods of relief, and enables the puppies to explore different surroundings. This experience paves the way for a less traumatic event when the pups eventually are crated.

At four to five weeks of age, place two or three puppies together in a single crate for about five to ten minutes at a time, two or three times a day. As the puppies grow accustomed to the crate, increase the length of the stay. You can start feeding them in the crate, and they will associate the food experience with going into the crate. By the time they are weaned, they should be well adjusted.

Finally, start taking the dogs for short rides in the car. Have someone hold them and comfort them during the ride. Later, introduce them to the crate in the car with assurances and rewards.

HOUSEBREAKING

Puppies do not begin to exercise some voluntary control over their bladder and bowel functions until they reach five weeks of age. The average dog takes five to six weeks to housebreak. Full bladder control may take somewhat longer. Normally a puppy that is 8 to 12 weeks of age is expected to have a nature call every two hours. Success in housebreaking depends on whether you, the dog owner, can be trained. Any failure in housebreaking is usually the owner's fault. Puppies have a natural instinct to avoid soiling their sleeping quarters. This is to your advantage in housebreaking.

Your puppy will have a routine that you may as well get accustomed to and incorporate into your daily living. Pups usually eliminate almost immediately after eating, so develop a three-time-a-day feeding routine, feeding the same food at the same time in the same place. Additionally, after a nap and after playing are also times when the pup will have to eliminate. Add to these times two other times that meet your schedule. Make sure to take the pup out *first thing* in the morning and *last thing* at night. When you take him outdoors, take him to the same place each time. When the pup voids, give him praise, pets and treats.

Contrary to popular belief, rubbing your puppy's nose in his mistakes indoors is counterproductive to the training and should not be done. Even if caught in the act, the puppy's natural reaction is to assume that you object to him going to the bathroom. In fact, you are not objecting to the natural function, but to the *place* where the puppy has voided. This approach may inhibit a dog from going in the house (at least in your presence), but it causes confusion, apprehension and anxiety. Instead, when the puppy starts to whimper, puts his nose to the ground and runs around looking restless, take him outside or to the paper before the accident happens. It is much better to teach him the right way than to punish him for what you term as misbehaving. If he starts to misbehave in the house without asking to go out first, scold him and take him out or to the paper. Punishment after the

Dogs do not like to soil where they sleep and therefore will do their very best not to soil in their crate. Provide your Chinese Crested with plenty of time out of his crate to do his business, and you will not have a problem.

fact will accomplish nothing; the puppy cannot understand why he is being scolded unless it is immediate. A dog does not use reason, as it is an animal of habit. *You* are expected to use reasoning. Exercise patience and redirect his behavior into an acceptable behavior.

If for some reason you have to be gone from home for a period of time, such as work, you can use newspapers as the voiding area in the home. First, confine *When paper training your Chinese Crested puppy, take him to his paper after he awakes from a nap, after meals, and anytime he puts his nose to the ground and runs around looking restless.*

the pup in a *small* area and line the floor with newspapers away from his sleeping area or pad. Use several thicknesses, and afterward you can remove the soiled papers from the top and add clean newspapers on top. The middle layer will retain some odor as a reminder to the pup to use that area. Later, as the puppy gains more control and has developed a routine of going outside, you can remove the newspapers when you come home and clean and disinfect the floor thoroughly.

Once you have established a solid routine, the use of a crate is almost imperative in maintaining housebreaking and retention of the house rules. You may have used the bathroom, a corner of the basement or a spot in the kitchen for confinement during the training period, along with the paper method. You may have already introduced the crate, or you should begin using it for confinement as your next step. Place the pup in a crate at night or when you are gone for more than six hours. The crate should be large enough for the pup to lay down; any larger and the pup will soil his bedding in the corner.

To pick the correct size crate, you must consider how big the dog will be when full-grown. The length of the crate should allow approximately 6 to 12 inches stretching space for the lying dog. This way you only buy one crate. While the dog is still growing, the crate can be made smaller by using a wood partition or panel that leaves just enough space for the dog to lie down. The crate will become the dog's security at home and away from home when traveling.

As a rule, females are housebroken more easily. They relieve themselves more modestly and require less shrubbery and trees than males. The male is more anxious to roam, looking for adventure and sex.

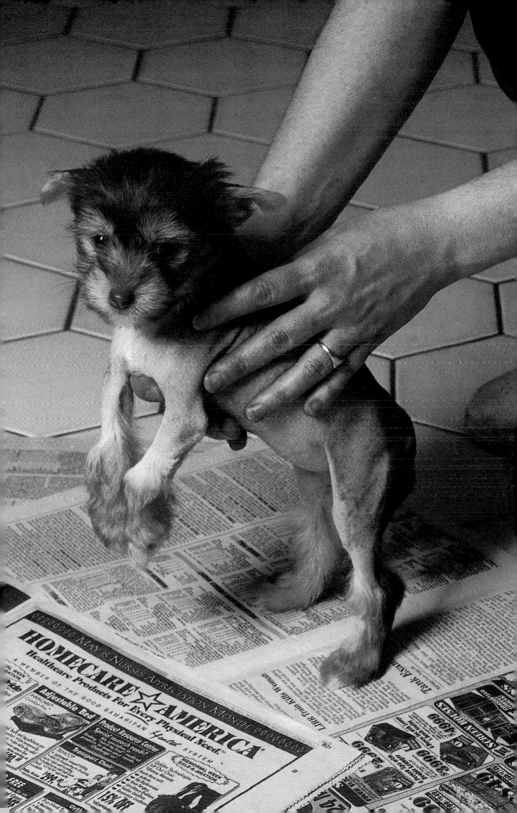

SPORT of Purebred Dogs

elcome to the exciting and sometimes frustrating sport of dogs. No doubt you are trying to learn more about dogs or you wouldn't be deep into this book. This section covers the basics that may entice you, further your knowledge and help you to understand the dog world.

Dog showing has been a very popular sport for a long time and has been taken quite seriously by some. Others only enjoy it as a hobby.

The Kennel Club in England was formed in 1859, the American Kennel Club was established in 1884 and the Canadian Kennel Club was formed in 1888. The purpose of these clubs was to register purebred dogs and maintain their Stud Books. In the beginning, the concept of registering dogs was not readily accepted. More than 36 million dogs have been enrolled in the AKC Stud Book since its inception in 1888. Presently the kennel clubs not only register dogs but adopt and enforce rules and regulations governing dog shows, obedience trials and field trials. Over the years they have fostered and encouraged interest in the health and welfare of the purebred dog. They routinely donate funds to veterinary research for study on genetic disorders.

Below are the addresses of the kennel clubs in the United States, Great Britain and Canada.

Conformation showing judges your dog on how closely he conforms to the standard of the breed.

Posing their show dogs in the most flattering positions to emphasize the dog's strengths and hide flaws is what professional handlers do best, and is what wins shows.

The American Kennel Club
51 Madison Avenue
New York, NY 10010
(Their registry is located at:
5580 Centerview Drive, STE
200, Raleigh, NC 27606-3390)

The Kennel Club
1 Clarges Street
Piccadilly, London, WIY 8AB, England

The Canadian Kennel Club
111 Eglinton Avenue
East Toronto, Ontario M6S 4V7
Canada

Today there are numerous activities that are enjoyable for both the dog and the handler. Some of the activities include conformation showing, obedience competition, tracking, agility, the Canine Good Citizen Certificate, and a wide range of instinct tests that vary from breed to breed. Where you start depends upon your goals which early on may not be readily apparent.

PUPPY KINDERGARTEN

Every puppy will benefit from this class. PKT is the foundation for all future dog activities from conformation to "couch potatoes." Pet owners should make an effort to attend even if they never expect to show their dog. The class is designed for puppies about three months of age with graduation at approximately five months of age. All the puppies will be in the same age group and, even though some may be a little unruly, there should not be any real problem. This class will teach the puppy some beginning obedience. As in all obedience classes the owner learns how to train his own dog. The PKT class gives the puppy the opportunity to interact with other puppies in the same age group and exposes him to strangers, which is very important. Some dogs grow up with behavior problems, one of them being fear of strangers. As you can see, there can be much to gain from this class.

All Chinese Crested puppies can benefit from early training to teach them basic obedience and good manners.

There are some basic obedience exercises that every dog should learn. Some of these can be started with puppy kindergarten.

Sit

One way of teaching the sit is to have your dog on your left side with the leash in your right hand, close to the collar. Pull up on the leash and at the same time reach around his hindlegs with your left hand and tuck them in. As you are doing this say, "Beau, sit." Always use the dog's name when you give an active command. Some owners like to use a treat holding it over the

One of the basic commands that every dog should know is the "Sit."

dog's head. The dog will need to sit to get the treat.

Encourage the dog to hold the sit for a few seconds, which will eventually be the beginning of the Sit/Stay. Depending on how cooperative he is, you can rub him under the chin or stroke his back. It is a good time to establish eye contact.

Down

Sit the dog on your left side and kneel down beside him with the leash in your right hand. Reach over him with your left hand and grasp his left foreleg. With your right hand, take his right foreleg and pull his legs forward while you say, "Beau, down." If he tries to get up, lean on his shoulder to encourage him to stay down. It will relax your dog if you stroke his back while he is down. Try to encourage him to stay down for a few seconds as preparation for the Down/Stay.

Heel

The definition of heeling is the dog walking under control at your left heel. Your puppy will learn controlled walking in the puppy kindergarten class, which will eventually lead to heeling. The command is "Beau, heel," and you start off briskly with your left foot. Your leash is in your right hand and your left hand is holding it about half way down. Your left hand should be able to control the leash and there should be a little slack in it. You want him to walk with you with your leg somewhere between his nose and his shoulder. You need to encourage him to stay with you, not forging (in front of you) or lagging behind you. It is best to keep him on a fairly short lead. Do not allow the lead to become tight. It is far better to give him a little jerk when necessary and remind him to heel. When you come to a halt, be prepared physically to make him sit. It takes practice to become coordinated. There are excellent books on training that you may wish to purchase. Your instructor should be able to recommend one for you.

Recall

This quite possibly is the most important exercise you will ever teach. It should be a pleasant experience. The puppy may learn to do random recalls while being attached to a long line such as a clothes line. Later the exercise will start with the dog sitting and staying until called. The command is "Beau, come." Let your command be happy. You want your dog to come willingly and faithfully. The recall could save his life if he sneaks out the door. In practicing the recall, let him jump on you or touch you before you reach for him. If he is shy, then kneel down to his level. Reaching for the insecure dog could frighten him, and he may not be willing to come again in the future. Lots of praise and a treat would be in order whenever you do a recall. Under no circumstances should you ever correct your dog when he has come to you. Later in formal obedience your dog will be required to sit in front of you after recalling and then go to heel position.

CONFORMATION

Conformation showing is our oldest dog show sport. This type of showing is based on the dog's appearance–that is his structure, movement and attitude. When considering this type of showing, you need to be aware of your breed's standard and be able to evaluate your dog compared to that standard. The breeder of your puppy or other experienced breeders would be good sources for such an evaluation. Puppies can go through lots of changes over a period of time. Many puppies start out as promising hopefuls and then after maturing may be disappointing as show candidates. Even so this should not deter them from being excellent pets.

Usually conformation training classes are offered by the local kennel or obedience clubs. These are excellent places for training puppies. The puppy should be able to walk on a lead before entering such a class. Proper ring procedure

Successful showing requires dedication and preparation, but most of all, it should be an enjoyable experience for handlers and dogs alike.

and technique for posing (stacking) the dog will be
demonstrated as well as gaiting the dog. Usually certain
patterns are used in the ring such as the triangle or the "L."
Conformation class, like the PKT class, will give your
youngster the opportunity to socialize
with different breeds of dogs and
humans too.

*Ch. Gingery's Lord
of the Rings,
"Ringo," owned by
Sherry Cleveland.*

It takes some time to learn the routine
of conformation showing. Usually one
starts at the puppy matches that may be
AKC Sanctioned or Fun Matches. These
matches are generally for puppies from two or three months to
a year old, and there may be classes for the adult over the age
of 12 months. Similar to point shows, the classes are divided by
sex and after completion of the classes in that breed or variety,
the class winners compete for Best of Breed or Variety. The
winner goes on to compete in the Group and the Group
winners compete for Best in Match. No championship points
are awarded for match wins.

A few matches can be great training for puppies even
though there is no intention to go on showing. Matches enable
the puppy to meet new people and be handled by a stranger—
the judge. It is also a change of environment, which broadens
the horizon for both dog and handler. Matches and other dog
activities boost the confidence of the handler and especially
the younger handlers.

Earning an AKC championship is built on a point system,
which is different from Great Britain. To become an AKC
Champion of Record the dog must earn 15 points. The number
of points earned each time depends upon the number of dogs
in competition. The number of points available at each show
depends upon the breed, its sex and the location of the show.
The United States is divided into ten AKC zones. Each zone has
its own set of points. The purpose of the zones is to try to
equalize the points available from breed to breed and area to
area.The AKC adjusts the point scale annually.

The number of points that can be won at a show are
between one and five. Three-, four- and five-point wins are
considered majors. Not only does the dog need 15 points won
under three different judges, but those points must include
two majors under two different judges. Canada also works on a

point system but majors are not required.

Dogs always show before bitches. The classes available to those seeking points are: Puppy (which may be divided into 6 to 9 months and 9 to 12 months); 12 to 18 months; Novice; Bred-by-Exhibitor; American-bred; and Open. The class winners of the same sex of each breed or variety compete against each other for Winners Dog and Winners Bitch. A Reserve Winners Dog and Reserve Winners Bitch are also awarded but do not carry any points unless the Winners win is disallowed by AKC. The Winners Dog and Bitch compete with the specials (those dogs that have attained championship) for Best of Breed or Variety, Best of Winners and Best of Opposite Sex. It is possible to pick up an extra point or even a major if the points are higher for the defeated winner than those of Best of Winners. The latter

Ch. Gingery's White Lion of Oz winning Best of Breed at the 1994 Chinese Crested Club of the Potomac Specialty.

would get the higher total from the defeated winner.

At an all-breed show, each Best of Breed or Variety winner will go on to his respective Group and then the Group winners will compete against each other for Best in Show. There are seven Groups: Sporting, Hounds, Working, Terriers, Toys, Non-Sporting and Herding. Obviously there are no Groups at speciality shows (those shows that have only one breed or a show such as the American Spaniel Club's Flushing Spaniel Show, which is for all flushing spaniel breeds).

Conformation showing allows an owner and/or handler to see how well their dog matches up to the standard.

Earning a championship in England is somewhat different since they do not have a point system. Challenge Certificates are awarded if the judge feels the dog is deserving regardless of the number of dogs in competition. A dog must earn three Challenge Certificates under three different judges, with at least one of these Certificates being won after the age of 12 months. Competition is very strong and entries may be higher than they are in the U.S. The Kennel Club's Challenge Certificates are only available at Championship Shows.

In England, The Kennel Club regulations require that certain dogs, Border Collies and Gundog breeds, qualify in a working capacity (i.e., obedience or field trials) before becoming a full Champion. If they do not qualify in the working aspect, then they are designated a Show Champion, which is equivalent to the AKC's Champion of Record. A Gundog may be granted the title of Field Trial Champion (FT Ch.) if it passes all the tests in the field but would also have to qualify in conformation before becoming a full Champion. A Border Collie that earns the title of Obedience Champion (Ob Ch.) must also qualify in the conformation ring before becoming a Champion.

The U.S. doesn't have a designation full Champion but does award for Dual and Triple Champions. The Dual Champion must be a Champion of Record, and either Champion Tracker, Herding Champion, Obedience Trial Champion or Field Champion. Any dog that has been awarded the titles of Champion of Record, and any two of the following: Champion Tracker, Herding Champion, Obedience Trial Champion or Field Champion, may be designated as a Triple Champion.

The shows in England seem to put more emphasis on breeder judges than those in the U.S. There is much competition within the

Attitude is just as important on the dog's part as it is on the part of the handler. A positive and happy attitude is important to have during conformation showing.

breeds. Therefore the quality of the individual breeds should be very good. In the United States we tend to have more "all around judges" (those that judge multiple breeds) and use the breeder judges at the specialty shows. Breeder judges are more familiar with their own breed since they are actively breeding that breed or did so at one time. Americans emphasize Group and Best in Show wins and promote them accordingly.

The shows in England can be very large and extend over several days, with the Groups being scheduled on different days. Though multi-day shows are not common in the U.S., there are cluster shows, where several different clubs will use the same show site over consecutive days.

Westminster Kennel Club is our most prestigious show although the entry is limited to 2500. In recent years, entry has been limited to Champions. This show is more formal than the majority of the shows with the judges wearing formal attire and the

Ch. Gingery's Maple Syrup winning Best of Breed at the 1993 Westminster Kennel Club Show.

BEST OF
BREED
Clermont County
K.C.
MAY
1995 ©
Baines Photo

handlers fashionably dressed. In most instances the quality of the dogs is superb. After all, it is a show of Champions. It is a good show to study the AKC registered breeds and is by far the most exciting—especially since it is televised! WKC is one of the few shows in this country that is still benched. This means the dog must be in his benched area during the show hours except when he is being groomed, in the ring, or being exercised.

Typically, the handlers are very particular about their appearances. They are careful not to wear something that will detract from their dog but will perhaps enhance it. American ring procedure is quite formal compared to that of other countries.

Ch. Gingery's Krimson 'N' Clover, handled by Victor Helu, winning Group First at the 1997 Greater Lowell Kennel Club Show.

There is a certain etiquette expected between the judge and exhibitor and among the other exhibitors. Of course it is not always the case but the judge is supposed to be polite, not engaging in small talk or acknowledging how well he knows the handler. There is a more informal and relaxed atmosphere at the shows in other countries. For instance, the dress code is more casual. I can see where this might be more fun for the exhibitor and especially for the novice. The U.S. is very handler-oriented in many of the breeds. It is true, in most instances, that the experienced professional handler can present the dog better and will have a feel for what a judge likes.

In England, Crufts is The Kennel Club's own show and is most assuredly the largest dog show in the world. They've been known to have an entry of nearly 20,000, and the show lasts four days. Entry is only gained by qualifying through winning in specified classes at

Ch. Gingery's Cheesecake, owned by Arlene Butterklee and handled by Victor Helu, winning Best in Show at the 1992 South Bristol Kennel Club Show.

another Championship Show. Westminster is strictly conformation, but Crufts exhibitors and spectators enjoy not only conformation but obedience, agility and a multitude of exhibitions as well. Obedience was admitted in 1957 and agility in 1983.

If you are handling your own dog, please give some consideration to your apparel. For sure the dress code at matches is more informal than the point shows. However, you should wear something a little more appropriate than beach attire or ragged jeans and bare feet. If you check out the handlers and see what is presently fashionable, you'll catch on. Men usually dress with a shirt and tie and a nice sports coat. Whether you are male or female, you will want to wear comfortable clothes and shoes. You need to be able to run with your dog and you certainly don't want to take a chance of falling and hurting yourself. Heaven forbid, if nothing else, you'll upset your dog. Women usually wear a dress or two-piece outfit, preferably with pockets to carry bait, comb, brush, etc. In this case men are the lucky ones with all their pockets. Ladies, think about where your dress will be if you need to kneel on the floor and also think about running. Does it allow freedom to do so?

You need to take along dog; crate; ex pen (if you use one); extra newspaper; water pail and water; all required grooming equipment, including hair dryer and extension cord; table; chair for you; bait for dog and lunch for you and friends; and, last but not least, clean up materials, such as plastic bags, paper towels, and perhaps a bath towel and some shampoo—just in case. Don't forget your entry confirmation and directions to the show.

If you are showing in obedience, then you will want to wear pants. Many of our top obedience handlers wear pants that are color-coordinated with their dogs. The philosophy is that imperfections in the black dog will be less obvious next to your black pants.

Whether you are showing in conformation, Junior Showmanship or obedience, you need to watch the clock and be sure you are not late. It is customary to pick up your conformation armband a few minutes before the start of the class. They will not wait for you and if you are on the show grounds and not in the ring, you will upset everyone. It's a little more complicated picking up your obedience armband if you show later in the class. If you have not picked up your armband and they get to your number, you may not be allowed to show. It's best to pick up your armband early, but then you may show earlier than expected if other handlers don't pick up. Customarily all conflicts should be discussed with the judge prior to the start of the class.

Junior Showmanship

Crufts Dog Show is England's most important show. Handlers and their dogs have a large competition field,— nearly 20,000 dogs are entered over four days of showing.

The Junior Showmanship Class is a wonderful way to build self confidence even if there are no aspirations of staying with the dog-show game later in life. Frequently, Junior Showmanship becomes the background of those who become successful exhibitors/ handlers in the future. In some instances it is taken very seriously, and success is measured in terms of wins. The Junior Handler is judged solely on his ability and skill in presenting his dog. The dog's conformation is not to be considered by the judge. Even so the condition and grooming of the dog may be a reflection upon the handler.

Usually the matches and point shows include different classes. The Junior Handler's dog may be entered in a breed or obedience class and even shown by another person in that class. Junior Showmanship classes are usually divided by age and perhaps sex. The age is determined by the handler's age on the day of the show. The classes are:

Novice Junior for those at least ten and under 14 years of age who at time of entry closing have not won three first places in a Novice Class at a licensed or member show.

Novice Senior for those at least 14 and under 18 years of

101

age who at the time of entry closing have not won three first places in a Novice Class at a licensed or member show.

Open Junior for those at least ten and under 14 years of age who at the time of entry closing have won at least three first places in a Novice Junior Showmanship Class at a licensed or member show with competition present.

Open Senior for those at least 14 and under 18 years of age who at time of entry closing have won at least three first places in a Novice Junior Showmanship Class at a licensed or member show with competition present.

Junior Handlers must include their AKC Junior Handler number on each show entry. This needs to be obtained from the AKC.

CANINE GOOD CITIZEN

The AKC sponsors a program to encourage dog owners to train their dogs. Local clubs perform the pass/fail tests, and dogs who pass are awarded a Canine Good Citizen Certificate. Proof of vaccination is required at the time of participation. The test includes:

1. Accepting a friendly stranger.
2. Sitting politely for petting.
3. Appearance and grooming.
4. Walking on a loose leash.
5. Walking through a crowd.
6. Sit and down on command/staying in place.
7. Come when called.
8. Reaction to another dog.
9. Reactions to distractions.
10. Supervised separation.

Good manners are paramount, but appearance and grooming are all important when earning a Canine Good Citizen Certificate.

If more effort was made by pet owners to accomplish these exercises, fewer dogs would be cast off to the humane shelter.

OBEDIENCE

Obedience is necessary, without a doubt, but it can also become a wonderful hobby or even an obsession. Obedience classes and competition can provide wonderful companionship, not only with your dog but with your classmates or fellow competitors. It is always gratifying to discuss your dog's problems with others who have had similar

Winning awards is very rewarding for both dog and owner. The Chinese Crested is becoming a very popular breed, and therefore competition is very challenging.

experiences. The AKC acknowledged Obedience around 1936, and it has changed tremendously even though many of the exercises are basically the same. Today, obedience competition is just that—very competitive. Even so, it is possible for every obedience exhibitor to come home a winner (by earning qualifying scores) even though he/she may not earn a placement in the class.

Most of the obedience titles are awarded after earning three qualifying scores (legs) in the appropriate class under three different judges. These classes offer a perfect score of 200, which is extremely rare. Each of the class exercises has its own point value. A leg is earned after receiving a score of at least 170 and at least 50 percent of the points available in each exercise. The titles are:

Companion Dog–CD

This is called the Novice Class and the exercises are:

1. Heel on leash and figure 8	40 points
2. Stand for examination	30 points
3. Heel free	40 points
4. Recall	30 points

5. Long sit—one minute   30 points
6. Long down—three minutes   30 points
Maximum total score   200 points

Companion Dog Excellent—CDX
This is the Open Class and the exercises are:
1. Heel off leash and figure 8   40 points
2. Drop on recall   30 points
3. Retrieve on flat   20 points
4. Retrieve over high jump   30 points
5. Broad jump   20 points
6. Long sit—three minutes (out of sight) 30 points
7. Long down—five minutes (out of sight) 30 points
Maximum total score   200 points

Utility Dog—UD
The Utility Class exercises are:
1. Signal Exercise   40 points
2. Scent discrimination-Article 1   30 points
3. Scent discrimination-Article 2   30 points
4. Directed retrieve   30 points
5. Moving stand and examination   30 points
6. Directed jumping   40 points
Maximum total score   200 points

After achieving the UD title, you may feel inclined to go after the UDX and/or OTCh. The UDX (Utility Dog Excellent) title went into effect in January 1994. It is not easily attained. The title requires qualifying simultaneously ten times in Open B and Utility B but not necessarily at consecutive shows.

The OTCh (Obedience Trial Champion) is awarded after the dog has earned his UD and then goes on to earn 100 championship points, a first place in Utility, a first place in Open and another first place in either class. The

These two beautiful Chinese Cresteds look like they are ready for any challenge thrown their way.

placements must be won under three different judges at all-breed obedience trials. The points are determined by the number of dogs competing in the Open B and Utility B classes. The OTCh title precedes the dog's name.

Obedience matches (AKC Sanctioned, Fun, and Show and Go) are usually available. Usually they are sponsored by the local obedience clubs. When preparing an obedience dog for a title, you will find matches very helpful. Fun Matches and Show and Go Matches are more lenient in allowing you to make corrections in the ring. This type of training is usually very necessary for the Open and Utility Classes. AKC Sanctioned Obedience Matches do not allow corrections

In conformation showing, handlers gait their dogs around the ring so that the judge can evaluate the dog's movement.

The dog show world is a busy life. Sometimes owners and handlers must travel great distances within short periods of time to arrive at the next show.

in the ring since they must abide by the AKC Obedience Regulations. If you are interested in showing in obedience, then you should contact the AKC for a copy of the Obedience Regulations.

HEALTH CARE

Veterinary medicine has become far more sophisticated than what was available to our ancestors. This can be attributed to the increase in household pets and consequently the demand for better care for them. Also human medicine has become far more complex. Today diagnostic testing in veterinary medicine parallels human diagnostics. Because of better technology we can expect our pets to live healthier lives thereby increasing their life spans.

THE FIRST CHECK UP

You will want to take your new puppy/dog in for its first check up within 48 to 72 hours after acquiring it. Many breeders strongly recommend this check up and so do the humane shelters. A puppy/dog can appear healthy but it may have a serious problem that is not apparent to the layman. Most pets have some type of a minor flaw that may never cause a real problem.

Puppies receive maternal antibodies for certain diseases but they are usually gone by 12 weeks of age. Immunizations are begun early to provide immunity when these run out.

Unfortunately if he/she should have a serious problem, you will want to consider the consequences of keeping the pet and the attachments that will be formed, which may be broken prematurely. Keep in mind there are many healthy dogs looking for good homes.

This first check up is a good time to establish yourself with the veterinarian and learn the office policy regarding their hours and how they handle emergencies. Usually the breeder or another conscientious pet owner is a good reference for

By breeding only the best quality dogs, good health and temperament is passed down to each new generation.

locating a capable veterinarian. You should be aware that not all veterinarians give the same quality of service. Please do not make your selection on the least expensive clinic, as they may be short changing your pet. There is the possibility that eventually it will cost you more due to improper diagnosis, treatment, etc. If you are selecting a new veterinarian, feel free to ask for a tour of the clinic. You should inquire about making an appointment for a tour since all clinics are working clinics, and therefore may not be available all day for sightseers. You may worry less if you see where your pet will be spending the day if he ever needs to be hospitalized.

THE PHYSICAL EXAM

Your veterinarian will check your pet's overall condition, which includes listening to the heart; checking the respiration; feeling the abdomen, muscles and joints; checking the mouth, which includes the gum color and signs of gum disease along with plaque buildup; checking the ears for signs of an infection or ear mites; examining the eyes; and, last but not least, checking the condition of the skin and coat.

He should ask you questions regarding your pet's eating and elimination habits and invite you to relay your questions. It is a good idea to prepare a list so as not to forget anything. He should discuss the proper diet and the quantity to be fed. If this should differ from your breeder's recommendation, then you should convey to him the breeder's choice and see if he approves. If he recommends changing the diet, then this should be done over a few days so as not to cause a gastrointestinal upset. It is customary to take in a fresh stool

Puppies are very vulnerable when they are first born. They should see a veterinarian for a check-up within 48 to 72 hours of their birth.

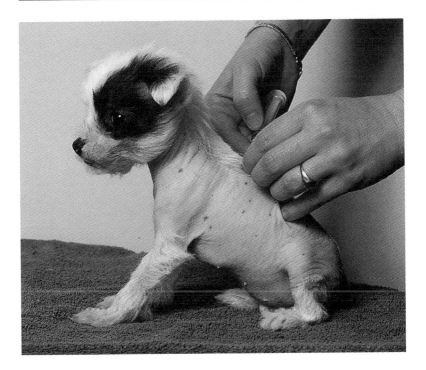

Find out which vaccinations your puppy has received prior to your bringing him home, for his health as well as the health of your family.

sample (just a small amount) for a test for intestinal parasites. It must be fresh, preferably within 12 hours, since the eggs hatch quickly and after hatching will not be observed under the microscope. If your pet isn't obliging then, usually the technician can take one in the clinic.

IMMUNIZATIONS

It is important that you take your puppy/dog's vaccination record with you on your first visit. In case of a puppy, presumably the breeder has seen to the vaccinations up to the time you acquired custody. Veterinarians differ in their vaccination protocol. It is not unusual for your puppy to have received vaccinations for distemper, hepatitis, leptospirosis, parvovirus and parainfluenza every two to three weeks from the age of five or six weeks. Usually this is a combined injection and is typically called the DHLPP. The DHLPP is given

A change in your Chinese Crested's behavior may indicate a health problem. See your veterinarian immediately if you suspect something is wrong.

through at least 12 to 14 weeks of age, and it is customary to continue with another parvovirus vaccine at 16 to 18 weeks. You may wonder why so many immunizations are necessary. No one knows for sure when the puppy's maternal antibodies are gone, although it is customarily accepted that distemper antibodies are gone by 12 weeks. Usually parvovirus antibodies are gone by 16 to 18 weeks of age. However, it is possible for the maternal antibodies to be gone at a much earlier age or even a later age. Therefore immunizations are started at an early age. The vaccine will not give immunity as long as there are maternal antibodies.

The rabies vaccination is given at three or six months of age depending on your local laws. A vaccine for bordetella (kennel cough) is advisable and can be given anytime from the age of five weeks. The coronavirus is not commonly given unless there is a problem locally. The Lyme vaccine is necessary in endemic areas. Lyme disease has been reported in 47 states.

Distemper

This is virtually an incurable disease. If the dog recovers, he is subject to severe nervous disorders. The virus attacks every tissue in the body and resembles a bad cold with a fever. It can cause a runny nose and eyes and cause gastrointestinal disorders, including a poor appetite, vomiting and diarrhea. The virus is carried by raccoons, foxes, wolves, mink and other dogs. Unvaccinated youngsters and senior citizens are very susceptible. This is still a common disease.

Many viral infections can be acquired when dogs are kept in close quarters. Make sure that your Chinese Crested is healthy and properly vaccinated.

Hepatitis

This is a virus that is most serious in very young dogs. It is spread by contact with an infected animal or its stool or urine. The virus affects the liver and kidneys and is characterized by high fever, depression and lack of appetite. Recovered animals may be afflicted with chronic illnesses.

Leptospirosis

This is a bacterial disease transmitted by contact with the urine of an infected dog, rat or other wildlife. It produces severe symptoms of fever, depression, jaundice and internal bleeding and was fatal before the vaccine was developed. Recovered dogs can be carriers, and the disease can be transmitted from dogs to humans.

Parvovirus

This was first noted in the late 1970s and is still a fatal disease. However, with proper vaccinations, early diagnosis and prompt treatment, it is a manageable disease. It attacks the bone marrow and intestinal tract. The symptoms include depression, loss of appetite, vomiting, diarrhea and collapse. Immediate medical attention is of the essence.

Rabies

This is shed in the saliva and is carried by raccoons, skunks, foxes, other dogs and cats. It attacks nerve tissue, resulting in paralysis and death. Rabies can be transmitted to people and is virtually always fatal. This disease is reappearing in the suburbs.

Bordetella (Kennel Cough)

The symptoms are coughing, sneezing, hacking and retching accompanied by nasal discharge usually lasting from a few days to several weeks. There are several disease-producing organisms responsible for this disease. The present vaccines are helpful but do not protect for all the strains. It usually is not life threatening but in some instances it can progress to a serious bronchopneumonia. The disease is highly contagious. The vaccination should be given routinely for dogs that come in contact with other dogs, such as through boarding, training class or visits to the groomer.

Coronavirus

This is usually self limiting and not life threatening. It was first noted in the late '70s about a year before parvovirus. The virus produces a yellow/brown stool and there may be depression, vomiting and diarrhea.

Lyme Disease

This was first diagnosed in the United States in 1976 in Lyme, CT in people who lived in close proximity to the deer tick. Symptoms may include acute lameness, fever, swelling of joints and loss of appetite. Your veterinarian can advise you if you live in an endemic area.

After your puppy has completed his puppy vaccinations, you will continue to booster the DHLPP once a year. It is customary to booster the rabies one year after the first vaccine and then, depending on where you live, it should be boostered every year or every three years. This depends on your local laws. The Lyme and corona vaccines are boostered annually and it is recommended that the bordetella be boostered every six to eight months.

ANNUAL VISIT

I would like to impress the importance of the annual check up, which would include the booster vaccinations, check for intestinal parasites and test for heartworm. Today in our very busy world it is rush, rush and see "how much you can get for how little." Unbelievably, some non-veterinary businesses have entered into the vaccination business. More harm than good can come to your dog through improper vaccinations, possibly from inferior vaccines and/or the wrong schedule. More than likely you truly care about your companion dog and over the years you have devoted much time and expense to his well being. Perhaps you are unaware that a vaccination is not just a vaccination. There is more involved. Please, please follow through with regular physical examinations. It is so important for your veterinarian to know your dog and this is especially

Your Chinese Crested will be given an annual examination of his eyes, ears, heart, skin, coat and teeth. To keep his teeth in good shape all year round be sure to supply plenty of Nylabone® chew products.

true during middle age through the geriatric years. More than likely your older dog will require more than one physical a year. The annual physical is good preventive medicine. Through early diagnosis and subsequent treatment your dog can maintain a longer and better quality of life.

INTESTINAL PARASITES

Hookworms

These are almost microscopic intestinal worms that can cause anemia and therefore serious problems, including death, in young puppies. Hookworms can be transmitted to humans through penetration of the skin. Puppies may be born with them.

Roundworms

These are spaghetti-like worms that can cause a potbellied appearance and dull coat along with more severe symptoms, such as vomiting, diarrhea and coughing. Puppies acquire these while in the mother's uterus and through lactation. Both hookworms and roundworms may be acquired through ingestion.

Whipworms

These have a three-month life cycle and are not acquired through the dam. They cause intermittent diarrhea usually with mucus. Whipworms are possibly the most difficult worm to eradicate. Their eggs are very resistant to most environmental factors and can last for years until the proper conditions enable

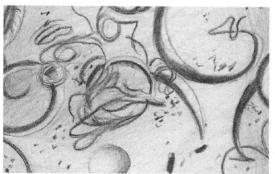

them to mature. Whipworms are seldom seen in the stool.

Whipworms are hard to find, and it is a job best left to a veterinarian. Pictured here are adult whipworms.

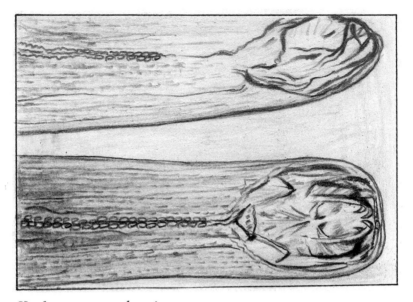

Hookworms are almost microscopic intestinal worms that can cause anemia and therefore serious problems, and even death.

Intestinal parasites are more prevalent in some areas than others. Climate, soil and contamination are big factors contributing to the incidence of intestinal parasites. Eggs are passed in the stool, lay on the ground and then become infective in a certain number of days. Each of the above worms has a different life cycle. Your best chance of becoming and remaining worm-free is to always pooper-scoop your yard. A fenced-in yard keeps stray dogs out, which is certainly helpful.

I would recommend having a fecal examination on your dog twice a year or more often if there is a problem. If your dog has a positive fecal sample, then he will be given the appropriate medication and you will be asked to bring back another stool sample in a certain period of time (depending on the type of worm) and then be rewormed. This process goes on until he has at least two negative samples. The different types of worms require different medications. You will be wasting your money and doing your dog an injustice by buying over-the-counter medication without first consulting your veterinarian.

OTHER INTERNAL PARASITES

Coccidiosis and Giardiasis

These protozoal infections usually affect puppies, especially in places where large numbers of puppies are brought together. Older dogs may harbor these infections but do not show signs unless they are stressed. Symptoms include diarrhea, weight loss and lack of appetite. These infections are not always apparent in the fecal examination.

Tapeworms

Seldom apparent on fecal floatation, they are diagnosed frequently as rice-like segments around the dog's anus and the base of the tail. Tapeworms are long, flat and ribbon like, sometimes several feet in length, and made up of many segments about five-eighths of an inch long. The two most common types of tapeworms found in the dog are:

Regular medical care is just as important for the adult Crested as it is for the puppy. Vaccination boosters and physical exams are part of your dog's lifelong maintenance.

(1) First the larval form of the flea tapeworm parasite must mature in an intermediate host, the flea, before it can become infective. Your dog acquires this by ingesting the flea through licking and chewing.

(2) Rabbits, rodents and certain large game animals serve as intermediate hosts for other species of tapeworms. If your dog should eat one of these infected hosts, then he can acquire tapeworms.

HEARTWORM DISEASE

This is a worm that resides in the heart and adjacent blood vessels of the lung that produces microfilaria, which circulate in the bloodstream. It is possible for a dog to be infected with any number of worms from one to a hundred that can

Dirofilaria—adult worms in the heart of a dog. It is possible for a dog to be infected with any number of worms from one to a hundred. Courtesy of Merck AgVet.

be 6 to 14 inches long. It is a life-threatening disease, expensive to treat and easily prevented. Depending on where you live, your veterinarian may recommend a preventive year-round and either an annual or semiannual blood test. The most common preventive is given once a month.

EXTERNAL PARASITES

Fleas

These pests are not only the dog's worst enemy but also enemy to the owner's pocketbook. Preventing is less expensive than treating, but regardless we'd prefer to spend our money elsewhere. Likely, the majority of our dogs are allergic to the bite of a flea, and in many cases it only takes one flea bite. The protein in the flea's saliva is the culprit. Allergic dogs have a reaction, which usually results in a "hot spot." More than likely such a reaction will involve a trip to the veterinarian for treatment. Yes, prevention is less expensive. Fortunately today there are several good products available.

If there is a flea infestation, no one product is going to correct the problem. Not only will the dog require treatment so will the environment. In general flea collars are not very effective although there is now available an "egg" collar that will kill the eggs on the dog. Dips are the most economical but they are messy. There are some effective shampoos and treatments available through pet shops and veterinarians. An oral tablet arrived on the American market in 1995 and was popular in Europe the previous year. It sterilizes the female flea but will not kill adult fleas. Therefore the tablet, which is given monthly, will decrease the flea population but is not a "cure-all." Those dogs that suffer from flea-bite allergy will still be subjected to the bite of the flea. Another popular parasiticide is permethrin, which is applied to the back of the dog in one or two places depending on the dog's weight. This product works as a repellent causing the flea to get "hot feet" and jump off. Do not confuse this product with some of the organophosphates that are also applied to the dog's back.

Some products are not usable on young puppies. Treating fleas should be done under your veterinarian's guidance. Frequently it is necessary to combine products and the layman does not have the knowledge regarding possible toxicities. It is hard to believe but there are a few dogs that do have a natural resistance to fleas. Nevertheless it would be wise to treat all pets at the same time. Don't forget your cats. Cats just love to prowl the neighborhood and consequently return with unwanted guests.

Adult fleas live on the dog but their eggs drop off the dog into the environment. There they go through four larval stages before reaching adulthood, and thereby are able to jump back on the poor unsuspecting dog. The cycle resumes and takes between 21 to 28 days under ideal conditions. There are environmental products available that will kill both the adult fleas and the larvae.

The deer tick is the most common carrier of Lyme disease. Your veterinarian can advise you if you live in an endemic area. Photo courtesy of Virbac Laboratories, Inc., Fort Worth, Texas.

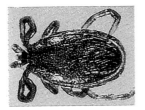

Ticks

Ticks carry Rocky Mountain Spotted Fever, Lyme disease and can cause tick paralysis. They should be removed with tweezers, trying to pull out the head. The jaws carry disease. There is a tick preventive collar that does an excellent job. The ticks automatically back out on those dogs wearing collars.

Sarcoptic Mange

This is a mite that is difficult to find on skin scrapings. The pinnal reflex is a good indicator of this disease. Rub the ends of the pinna (ear) together and the dog will start scratching with his foot. Sarcoptes are highly contagious to other dogs and to humans although they do not live long on humans. They cause intense itching.

Demodectic Mange

This is a mite that is passed from the dam to her puppies. It affects youngsters age three to ten months. Diagnosis is confirmed by skin scraping. Small areas of alopecia around the eyes, lips and/or forelegs become visible. There is little itching unless there is a secondary bacterial infection. Some breeds are afflicted more than others.

Cheyletiella

This causes intense itching and is diagnosed by skin scraping. It lives in the outer layers of the skin of dogs, cats, rabbits and humans. Yellow-gray scales may be found on the back and the rump, top of the head and the nose.

To Breed or Not To Breed

More than likely your breeder has requested that you have your puppy neutered or spayed. Your breeder's request is based on what is healthiest for your dog and what is most beneficial for your breed. Experienced and conscientious breeders devote many years into developing a bloodline. In order to do this, he makes every effort to plan each breeding in regard to conformation, temperament and health. This type of breeder does his best to perform the necessary testing (i.e., OFA, CERF, testing for inherited blood disorders, thyroid, etc.). Testing is expensive and sometimes very disheartening when a favorite dog doesn't pass his health tests. The health history pertains not only to the breeding stock but to the immediate ancestors. Reputable breeders do not

Breeding should only be attempted by someone who is conscientious, knowledgeable and willing to take responsibility for the dogs involved and the new puppies.

want their offspring to be bred indiscriminately. Therefore you may be asked to neuter or spay your puppy. Of course there is always the exception, and your breeder may agree to let you breed your dog under his direct supervision. This is an important concept. More and more effort is being made to breed healthier dogs.

Spay/Neuter

Having your Chinese Crested spayed or neutered eliminates the risk of cancer of the reproductive organs.

There are numerous benefits of performing this surgery at six months of age. Unspayed females are subject to mammary and ovarian cancer. In order to prevent mammary cancer she must be spayed prior to her first heat cycle. Later in life, an unspayed female may develop a pyometra (an infected uterus), which is definitely life threatening.

Spaying is performed under a general anesthetic and is easy on the young dog. As you might expect it is a little harder on the older dog, but that is no reason to deny her the surgery. The surgery removes the ovaries and uterus. It is important to remove all the ovarian tissue. If some is left behind, she could remain attractive to males. In order to view the ovaries, a reasonably long incision is necessary. An ovariohysterectomy is considered major surgery.

Neutering the male at a young age will inhibit some characteristic male behavior that owners frown upon.

Spaying/neutering is often the best option for your family pet. The health benefits are numerous and it will minimize the risk of certain diseases.

Some boys will not hike their legs and mark territory if they are neutered at six months of age. Also neutering at a young age has hormonal benefits, lessening the chance of hormonal aggressiveness.

Surgery involves removing the testicles but leaving the scrotum. If there should be a retained testicle, then he definitely needs to be neutered before the age of two or three years. Retained testicles can develop into cancer. Unneutered males are at risk for testicular cancer, perineal fistulas, perianal tumors and fistulas and prostatic disease.

Intact males and females are prone to housebreaking accidents. Females urinate frequently before, during and after heat cycles, and males tend to mark territory if there is a female in heat. Males may show the same behavior if there is a visiting dog or guests.

All Chinese Cresteds are cute, but not all are of breeding quality. Breeders usually sell pet quality puppies with the requirement that the puppies are spayed or neutered.

Surgery involves a sterile operating procedure equivalent to human surgery. The incision site is shaved, surgically scrubbed and draped. The veterinarian wears a sterile surgical gown, cap, mask and gloves. Anesthesia should be monitored by a registered technician. It is customary for the veterinarian to recommend a pre-anesthetic blood screening, looking for metabolic problems and a ECG rhythm strip to check for normal heart function. Today anesthetics are equal to human anesthetics, which enables your dog to walk out of the clinic the same day as surgery.

Some folks worry about their dog gaining weight after being neutered or spayed. This is usually not the case. It is true that some dogs may be less active so they could develop a problem, but most dogs are just as active as they were before surgery. However, if your dog should begin to gain, then you need to decrease his food and see to it that he gets a little more exercise.

Medical Problems

Anal Sacs

These are small sacs on either side of the rectum that can cause the dog discomfort when they are full. They should empty when the dog has a bowel movement. Symptoms of inflammation or impaction are excessive licking under the tail and/or a bloody or sticky discharge from the anal area. Breeders like myself recommend emptying the sacs on a regular schedule when bathing the dog. Many veterinarians prefer this isn't done unless there are symptoms. You can express the sacs by squeezing the two sacs (at the five and seven o'clock positions) in and up toward the anus. Take precautions not to get in the way of the foul-smelling fluid that is expressed. Some dogs object to this procedure so it would be wise to have someone hold the head. Scooting is caused by anal-sac irritation and not worms.

Given the proper blend of exercise, good nutrition, suitable housing, and routine veterinary care, your Chinese Crested can be expected to be an active member of your household for many years.

Colitis

The stool may be frank blood or blood tinged and is the result of inflammation of the colon. Colitis, sometimes intermittent, can be the result of stress, undiagnosed whipworms, or perhaps idiopathic (no explainable reason). If intermittent bloody stools are an ongoing problem, you should probably feed a diet higher in fiber. Seek professional help if your dog feels poorly and/or the condition persists.

Conjunctivitis

Many breeds are prone to this problem. The conjunctiva is the pink tissue that lines the inner surface of the eyeball except the clear, transparent cornea. Irritating substances such as bacteria, foreign matter or chemicals can cause it to become reddened and swollen. It is important to keep any hair trimmed from around the eyes. Long hair stays damp and aggravates the problem. Keep the eyes cleaned with warm water and wipe away any matter that has accumulated in the

corner of the eyes. If the condition persists, you should see your veterinarian. This problem goes hand in hand with keratoconjunctivitis sicca.

Ear Infection

Otitis externa is an inflammation of the external ear canal that begins at the outside opening of the ear and extends inward to the eardrum. Dogs with pendulous ears are prone to this disease, but isn't it interesting that breeds with upright ears also have a high incidence of problems? Allergies, food and inhalent, along with hormonal problems, such as hypothyroidism, are major contributors to the disease. For those dogs which have recurring problems you need to investigate the underlying cause if you hope to cure them.

Be careful never to get water into the ears. Water provides a great medium for bacteria to grow. If your dog swims or you inadvertently get water into his ears, then use a drying agent. An at-home preparation would be to use equal parts of three-percent hydrogen peroxide and 70-percent rubbing alcohol. Another preparation is equal parts of white vinegar and water. Your veterinarian alternatively can provide a suitable product. When cleaning the ears, be careful of using cotton tip applicators since they make it easy to pack debris down into the canal. Only clean what you can see.

If your dog has an ongoing infection, don't be surprised if your veterinarian recommends sedating him and flushing his ears with a bulb syringe. Sometimes this needs to be done a few times to get the ear clean. The ear must be clean so that medication can come in contact with the canal. Be prepared to return for rechecks until the infection is gone. This may involve more flushings if the ears are very bad.

Clip your Chinese Crested's toenails if they begin to get too long. Be careful not to cut the quick, as this will hurt and bleed.

For chronic or recurring cases, your veterinarian may recommend thyroid testing, etc., and a hypoallergenic diet for a trial period of 10 to 12 weeks. Depending on your dog, it may be a good idea to see a dermatologist. Ears shouldn't be taken lightly. If the condition gets out of hand, then surgery may be necessary. Please ask your veterinarian to explain proper ear maintenance for your dog.

Routinely check your Chinese Crested's skin and coat, as well as ears, for parasites or infection.

Flea Bite Allergy

This is the result of a hypersensitivity to the bite of a flea and its saliva. It only takes one bite to cause the dog to chew or scratch himself raw. Your dog may need medical attention to ease his discomfort. You need to clip the hair around the "hot spot" and wash it with a mild soap and water and you may need to do this daily if the area weeps. Apply an antibiotic anti-inflammatory product. Hot spots can occur from other trauma, such as grooming.

Interdigital Cysts

Check for these on your dog's feet if he shows signs of lameness. They are frequently associated with staph infections and can be quite painful. A home remedy is to soak the infected foot in a solution of a half teaspoon of bleach in a couple of quarts of water. Do this two to three times a day for a couple of days. Check with your veterinarian for an alternative remedy; antibiotics usually work well. If there is a recurring problem, surgery may be required.

Lameness

It may only be an interdigital cyst or it could be a mat between the toes, especially if your dog licks his feet. Sometimes it is hard to determine which leg is affected. If he is holding up his leg, then you need to see your veterinarian.

Skin

Frequently poor skin is the result of an allergy to fleas, an inhalant allergy or food allergy. These types of problems usually result in a staph dermatitis. Dogs with food allergy usually show signs of severe itching and scratching. Some dogs with food allergies never once itch. Their only symptom is swelling of the ears with no ear infection. Food allergy may result in recurrent bacterial skin and ear infections. Your veterinarian or dermatologist will recommend a good restricted diet. It is not wise for you to hit and miss with different dog foods. Many of the diets offered over the counter are not the hypoallergenic diet you are led to believe. Dogs acquire allergies through exposure.

Chinese Cresteds, like all pets, rely on their owners for care. It is the responsibility of good owners to give them everything they need to live happy and healthy lives.

Inhalant allergies result in atopy, which causes licking of the feet, scratching the body and rubbing the muzzle. It may be seasonable. Your veterinarian or dermatologist can perform intradermal testing for inhalant allergies. If your dog should test positive, then a vaccine may be prepared. The results are very satisfying.

Tonsillitis

Usually young dogs have a higher incidence of this problem than the older ones. The older dogs have built up resistance. It is very contagious. Sometimes it is difficult to determine if it is tonsillitis or kennel cough since the symptoms are similar. Symptoms include fever, poor eating, swallowing with difficulty and retching up a white, frothy mucus.

If you have more than one Chinese Crested, they will enjoy playing with each other...not to mention keep you very busy.

DENTAL CARE for Your Dog's Life

The average puppy has 28 baby teeth. Puppies do not have molars. There are some breeds that do not have premolars or have less of them. With the Chinese Crested there are certain genetic dentition problems, especially in the Hairless variety. In the Crested, the Puffs require full dentition when grown, while the Hairless are not to be penalized for missing teeth.

When your puppy is teething its body needs calcium to strengthen the teeth. A simple solution is to give the puppy "Tums," which contain calcium. This also helps the body's bone structure. Milk is purportedly a good source of calcium, however feeding the dog milk as a supplement can cause the dog to have diarrhea.

Part of the show routine is having the judge look at and evaluate the dog's teeth and bite in relation to AKC standards for the breed. Most puppies dislike having their teeth looked at, so this also requires desensitization. When the puppy starts teething, take your finger and gently rub the teeth and gums. Repetition is the key. As the puppy grows and becomes accustomed to having his teeth and gums touched, hold his

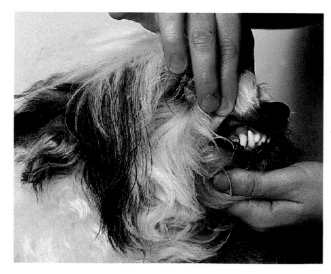

Each time your Chinese Crested has a physical exam, the veterinarian should thoroughly inspect his lips, teeth and gums.

mouth closed and raise his lips to show his bite. Once the pup is familiar with this, it won't be too distasteful an experience.

So you've got a new puppy! You also have a new set of puppy teeth in your household. Anyone who has ever raised a puppy is abundantly aware of these new teeth. Your puppy will chew anything it can reach, chase your shoelaces, and play "tear the rag" with any piece of clothing it can find. When puppies are newly born, they have no teeth. At about four weeks of age, puppies of most breeds begin to develop their deciduous or baby teeth. They begin eating semi-

2-Brush™ by Nylabone® is made with two toothbrushes to clean both sides of your dog's teeth at the same time. Each brush contains a reservoir designed to apply the toothpaste, which is especially formulated for dogs, directly to the toothbrush.

Toys, like Nylabones®, will help keep your Chinese Crested's teeth clean while keeping him busy and out of mischief.

solid food, fighting and biting with their litter mates, and learning discipline from their mother. As their new teeth come in, they inflict more pain on their mother's breasts, so her feeding sessions become less frequent and shorter. By six or eight weeks, the mother will start growling to warn her pups when they are fighting too roughly or hurting her as they nurse too much with their new teeth.

Puppies need to chew. It is a necessary part of their physical and mental development. They develop muscles and necessary life skills as they drag objects around, fight over possession, and vocalize alerts and warnings. Puppies chew on things to explore their world. They are using their sense of taste to determine what is food and what is not. How else can they tell an electrical cord from a lizard? At about four months of age, most puppies begin shedding their baby teeth. Often these teeth need some help to come out and make way for the permanent teeth. The incisors (front teeth) will be replaced first. Then, the adult canine or fang teeth erupt. When the baby tooth is not shed before the permanent tooth comes in, veterinarians call it a

To combat boredom and relieve your Chinese Crested's natural desire to chew, there's nothing better than a Roar-Hide™ from Nylabone®. Unlike common rawhide, this bone won't turn into a gooey mess when chewed on, so your dog won't choke on small pieces of it. The Roar-Hide™ is completely edible, high in protein and low in fat.

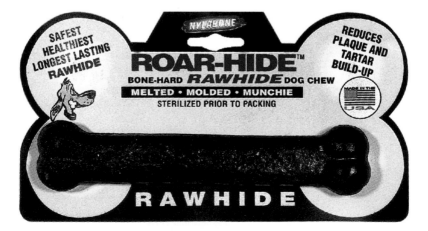

Your Chinese Crested will be happier and his teeth healthier if you give him a POPpup™ from Nylabone® to chew on. Every POPpup™ is 100% edible and enhanced with dog friendly ingredients like liver, cheese, spinach, chicken, carrots or potatoes. You can even microwave a POPpup™ to turn it into a crackly treat for your Chinese Crested to enjoy.

retained deciduous tooth. This condition will often cause gum infections by trapping hair and debris between the permanent tooth and the retained baby tooth. Nylafloss® is an excellent device for puppies to use. They can toss it, drag it, and chew on the many surfaces it presents. The baby teeth can catch in the nylon material, aiding in their removal. Puppies that have adequate chew toys will have less destructive behavior, develop more physically, and have less chance of retained deciduous teeth.

During the first year, your dog should be seen by your veterinarian at regular intervals. Your veterinarian will let you know when to bring in your puppy for vaccinations and parasite examinations. At each visit, your veterinarian should inspect the lips, teeth, and mouth as part of a complete physical examination. You should take some part in the maintenance of your dog's oral health. You should examine your dog's mouth weekly throughout his first year to make sure there are no sores, foreign objects, tooth problems, etc. If your dog drools excessively, shakes its head, or has bad breath, consult your veterinarian. By the

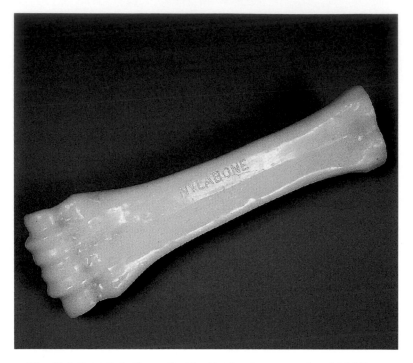

The Nylabone® is the only plastic dog bone made of 100% virgin nylon, specially processed to create a tough, durable, completely safe bone. As your Chinese Crested works a Nylabone®, he is strengthening his teeth and jaws.

time your dog is six months old, the permanent teeth are all in and plaque can start to accumulate on the tooth surfaces. This is when your dog needs to develop good dental-care habits to prevent calculus build-up on its teeth. Brushing is best. That is a fact that cannot be denied. However, some dogs do not like their teeth brushed regularly, or you may not be able to accomplish the task. In that case, you should consider a product that will help prevent plaque and calculus build-up.

The Plaque Attackers® and Galileo Bone® are other excellent choices for the first three years of a dog's life. Their shapes make them interesting for the dog. As the dog chews on them, the solid polyurethane massages the gums which improves the blood circulation to the periodontal tissues. Projections on the chew devices increase the surface and are in contact with the tooth for more efficient cleaning. The unique shape and consistency prevent your dog from exerting excessive force on his own teeth or from breaking off pieces of the bone. If your dog is an aggressive chewer or weighs more than 55 pounds (25 kg), you should consider giving him a Nylabone®, the most durable chew product on the market.

The Gumabones ®, made by the Nylabone Company, is constructed of strong polyurethane, which is softer than nylon. Less powerful chewers prefer the Gumabones® to the Nylabones®. A super option for your dog is the Hercules Bone®, a uniquely shaped bone named after the great Olympian for its exception strength. Like all Nylabone products, they are specially scented to make them attractive to your dog. Ask your veterinarian about these bones and he will validate the good doctor's prescription: Nylabones® not only give your dog a good chewing workout but also help to save your dog's teeth (and even his life, as it protects him from possible fatal periodontal diseases).

Take your Chinese Crested to the veterinarian for regular dental checkups so he can check for sores, tooth problems, and general oral health.

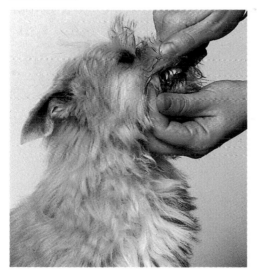

By the time dogs are four years old, 75% of them have periodontal disease. It is the most common infection in dogs. Yearly examinations by your veterinarian are essential to maintaining your dog's good health. If your veterinarian detects periodontal disease, he or she may recommend a prophylactic cleaning. To do a thorough cleaning, it will be necessary to put your dog under anesthesia. With modern gas anesthetics and monitoring equipment, the procedure is pretty safe. Your veterinarian will scale the teeth with an ultrasound scaler or hand instrument. This removes the calculus from the teeth. If there are calculus deposits below the gum line, the veterinarian will plane the roots to make them smooth. After all of the calculus has been removed, the teeth are polished with pumice in a polishing cup. If any medical or surgical treatment is needed, it is done at this time. The final step would be fluoride treatment and your follow-up treatment at home. If the periodontal disease is advanced, the veterinarian may prescribe a medicated mouth rinse or antibiotics for use at home. Make sure your dog has safe, clean and attractive chew toys and treats. Chooz® treats are another way of using a consumable

Teach your Chinese Crested constructive chewing habits by providing him with an array of Nylabone® products like Gumabones®.

treat to help keep your dog's teeth clean.

Rawhide is the most popular of all materials for a dog to chew. This has never been good news to dog owners, because rawhide is inherently very dangerous for dogs. Thousands of dogs have died from rawhide, having swallowed the hide after it has become soft and mushy, only to cause stomach and intestinal blockage. A new rawhide product on the market has finally solved the problem of rawhide: molded Roar-Hide™ from Nylabone. These are composed of processed, cut up, and melted American rawhide injected into your dog's favorite shape: a dog bone. These dog-safe devices smell and taste like rawhide but don't break up. The ridges on the bones help to fight tartar build-up on the teeth and they last ten times longer than the usual rawhide chews.

Carrots are rich in fiber, carbohydrates and vitamin A. The POPpup™ with carrots by Nylabone® is a durable chew containing no plastics or artificial ingredients and it can be served as is, in bone hard form, microwaved to a biscuity consistency.

As your dog ages, professional examination and cleaning should become more frequent. The mouth should be inspected at least once a year. Your veterinarian may recommend visits every six months. In the geriatric patient, organs such as the heart, liver, and kidneys do not function as well as when they were young. Your veterinarian will probably want to test these organs' functions prior to using general anesthesia for dental cleaning. If your dog is a good chewer and you work closely with your veterinarian, your dog can keep all of its teeth all of its life. However, as your dog ages, his sense of smell, sight, and taste will diminish. He may not have the desire to chase, trap or chew his toys. He will also not have the energy to chew for long periods, as arthritis and periodontal disease make chewing painful. This will leave you with more responsibility for keeping his teeth clean and healthy. The dog that would not let you brush his teeth at one year of age, may let you brush his teeth now that he is ten years old.

If you train your dog with good chewing habits as a puppy, he will have healthier teeth throughout his life.

TRAVELING with Your Dog

The earlier you start traveling with your new puppy or dog, the better. He needs to become accustomed to traveling. However, some dogs are nervous riders and become carsick easily. It is helpful if he starts with an empty stomach. Do not despair, as it will go better if you continue taking him with you on short fun rides. How would you feel if every time you rode in the car you stopped at the doctor's for an injection? You would soon dread that nasty car. Older dogs that tend to get carsick may have more of a problem adjusting to traveling. Those dogs that are having a serious problem may benefit from some medication prescribed by the veterinarian.

If you decide to bring your Chinese Crested with you when you travel, bring along some familiar things, like his toys and his crate, to make him feel at home.

Do give your dog a chance to relieve himself before getting into the car. It is a good idea to be prepared for a clean up with a leash, paper towels, bag and terry cloth towel.

The safest place for your dog is in a fiberglass crate, although close confinement can promote carsickness in some dogs. If your dog is nervous you can try letting him ride on the seat next to you or in someone's lap.

An alternative to the crate would be to use a car harness made for dogs and/or a safety strap attached to the harness or collar. Whatever you do, do not let your dog ride in the back of a pickup truck unless he is securely tied on a very short lead. I've seen trucks stop quickly and, even though the dog was tied, it fell out and was dragged.

Another advantage of the crate is that it is a safe place to leave him if you need to run into the store. Otherwise you wouldn't be able to leave the windows down. Keep in mind that while many dogs are overly protective in their crates, this may not be enough to deter dognappers. In some states it is against the law to leave a dog in the car unattended.

Never leave a dog loose in the car wearing a collar and leash. More than one dog has killed himself by hanging. Do not

let him put his head out an open window. Foreign debris can be blown into his eyes. When leaving your dog unattended in a car, consider the temperature. It can take less than five minutes to reach temperatures over 100 degrees Fahrenheit.

TRIPS

Perhaps you are taking a trip. Give consideration to what is best for your dog—traveling with you or boarding. When traveling by car, van or motor home, you need to think ahead about locking your vehicle. In all probability you have many valuables in the car and do not wish to leave it unlocked. Perhaps most valuable and not replaceable is your dog. Give thought to securing your vehicle and providing adequate ventilation for him. Another

When traveling with your Chinese Cresteds, always be certain to protect them when outdoors from the hot sun, as well as from the ground surface they are on.

consideration for you when traveling with your dog is medical problems that may arise and little inconveniences, such as exposure to external parasites. Some areas of the country are quite flea infested. You may want to carry flea spray with you. This is even a good idea when staying in motels. Quite possibly you are not the only occupant of the room.

Unbelievably many motels and even hotels do allow canine guests, even some very first-class ones. Gaines Pet Foods Corporation publishes *Touring With Towser*, a directory of domestic hotels and motels that accommodate guests with dogs. Their address is Gaines TWT, PO Box 5700, Kankakee, IL, 60902. Call ahead to any motel that you may be considering and see if they accept pets. Sometimes it is necessary to pay a deposit against room damage. The management may feel reassured if you mention that your dog will be crated. If you do

If you accustom your Chinese Crested to traveling when he is a puppy, he will be eager to follow you wherever you go!

travel with your dog, take along plenty of baggies so that you can clean up after him. When we all do our share in cleaning up, we make it possible for motels to continue accepting our pets. As a matter of fact, you should practice cleaning up everywhere you take your dog.

Depending on where your are traveling, you may need an up-to-date health certificate issued by your veterinarian. It is good policy to take along your dog's medical information, which would include the name, address and phone number of your veterinarian, vaccination record, rabies certificate, and any medication he is taking.

AIR TRAVEL

When traveling by air, you need to contact the airlines to check their policy. Usually you have to make arrangements up to a couple of weeks in advance for traveling with your dog. The airlines require your dog to travel in an airline approved fiberglass crate. Usually these can be purchased through the airlines but they are also readily available in most pet-supply stores. If your dog is not accustomed to a crate, then it is a good idea to get him acclimated to it before your trip. The day of the actual trip you should withhold water about one hour ahead of departure and no food for about 12 hours. The airlines generally have temperature restrictions, which do not allow pets to travel if it is either too cold or too hot. Frequently these restrictions are based on the temperatures at the departure and arrival airports. It's best to inquire about a health certificate. These usually need to be issued within ten days of departure. You should arrange for non-stop, direct flights and if a commuter plane should be involved, check to see if it will carry dogs. Some don't. The Humane Society of the United States has put together a tip sheet for airline traveling. You can receive a copy by sending a self-addressed stamped envelope to:

The Humane Society of the United States
Tip Sheet
2100 L Street NW
Washington, DC 20037.

Regulations differ for traveling outside of the country and are sometimes changed without notice. Well in advance you need to write or call the appropriate consulate or agricultural department for instructions. Some countries have lengthy quarantines (six months), and countries differ in their rabies vaccination requirements. For instance, it may have to be given at least 30 days ahead of your departure.

Do make sure your dog is wearing proper identification including your name, phone number and city. You never know when you might be in an accident and separated from your dog. Or your dog could be frightened and somehow manage to escape and run away.

Another suggestion would be to carry in-case-of-emergency instructions. These would include the address and phone number of a relative or friend, your veterinarian's name, address and phone number, and your dog's medical information.

BOARDING KENNELS

Perhaps you have decided that you need to board your dog. Your veterinarian can recommend a good boarding facility or possibly a pet sitter that will come to your house. It is customary for the boarding kennel to ask for proof of vaccination for the DHLPP, rabies and bordetella vaccine. The bordetella should have been given within six months of boarding. This is for your protection. If they do not ask for this proof I would not board at their kennel. Ask about flea control. Those dogs that suffer flea-bite allergy can get in trouble at a boarding kennel. Unfortunately boarding kennels are limited on how much they are able to do.

A reputable boarding kennel will require that dogs receive a vaccination for kennel cough no less than two weeks before their scheduled stay.

For more information on pet sitting, contact NAPPS: National Association of Professional Pet Sitters
1200 G Street, NW
Suite 760
Washington, DC 20005.

Some pet clinics have technicians that pet sit and technicians that board clinic patients in their homes. This may be an alternative for you. Ask your veterinarian if they have an employee that can help you. There is a definite advantage of having a technician care for your dog, especially if your dog is on medication or is a senior citizen.

You can write for a copy of *Traveling With Your Pet* from ASPCA, Education Department, 441 E. 92nd Street, New York, NY 10128.

IDENTIFICATION and Finding the Lost Dog

There are several ways of identifying your dog. The old standby is a collar with dog license, rabies, and ID tags. Unfortunately collars have a way of being separated from the dog and tags fall off. We're not suggesting you shouldn't use a collar and tags. If they stay intact and on the dog, they are the quickest way of identification.

For several years owners have been tattooing their dogs. Some tattoos use a number with a registry. Here lies the problem because there are several registries to check. If you wish to tattoo, use your social security number. The humane shelters have the means to trace it. It is usually done on the inside of the rear thigh. The area is first shaved and numbed. There is no pain, although a few dogs do not like the buzzing sound. Occasionally tattooing is not legible and needs to be redone.

The newest method of identification is microchipping. The microchip is a computer chip that is no larger than a grain of rice. The veterinarian implants it by injection between the shoulder blades. The dog feels no discomfort. If your dog is lost and picked up by the humane society, they can trace you by scanning the microchip, which has its own code. Microchip scanners are friendly to other brands of microchips and their registries. The microchip comes with a dog tag saying the dog is microchipped. It is the safest way of identifying your dog.

FINDING THE LOST DOG

I am sure you will agree that there would be little worse than losing your dog. Responsible pet owners rarely lose their

The newest method of identification is microchipping. The microchip is no bigger than a grain of rice.

dogs. They do not let their dogs run free because they don't want harm to come to them. Not only that but in most, if not all, states there is a leash law.

Beware of fenced-in yards. They can be a hazard. Dogs find ways to escape either over or under the fence. Another fast exit is through the gate that perhaps the neighbor's child left unlocked.

Make sure you have a clear, recent picture of your Chinese Crested to display in case he becomes lost.

Below is a list that hopefully will be of help to you if you need it. Remember don't give up, keep looking. Your dog is worth your efforts.

1. Contact your neighbors and put flyers with a photo on it in their mailboxes. Information you should include would be the dog's name, breed, sex, color, age, source of identification, when your dog was last seen and where, and your name and phone numbers. It may be helpful to say the dog needs medical care. Offer a *reward*.

2. Check all local shelters daily. It is also possible for your dog to be picked up away from home and end up in an out-of-the-way shelter. Check these too. Go in person. It is not good enough to call. Most shelters are limited on the time they can hold dogs then they are put up for adoption or euthanized. There is the possibility that your dog will not make it to the shelter for several days. Your dog could have been wandering or someone may have tried to keep him.

3. Notify all local veterinarians. Call and send flyers.

4. Call your breeder. Frequently breeders are contacted when one of their breed is found.

5. Contact the rescue group for your breed.

6. Contact local schools—children may have seen your dog.

7. Post flyers at the schools, groceries, gas stations, convenience stores, veterinary clinics, groomers and any other place that will allow them.

8. Advertise in the newspaper.

9. Advertise on the radio.

BEHAVIOR and Canine Communication

Studies of the human/animal bond point out the importance of the unique relationships that exist between people and their pets. Those of us who share our lives with pets understand the special part they play through companionship, service and protection. For many, the pet/owner bond goes beyond simple companionship; pets are often considered members of the family. A leading pet food manufacturer recently conducted a nationwide survey of pet owners to gauge just how important pets were in their lives. Here's what they found:

- 76 percent allow their pets to sleep on their beds
- 78 percent think of their pets as their children
- 84 percent display photos of their pets, mostly in their homes
- 84 percent think that their pets react to their own emotions
- 100 percent talk to their pets
- 97 percent think that their pets understand what they're saying

Are you surprised?

Senior citizens show more concern for their own eating habits when they have the responsibility of feeding a dog. Seeing that their dog is routinely exercised encourages the owner to think of schedules that otherwise may seem unimportant to the senior citizen. The older owner may be arthritic and feeling poorly but with responsibility for his dog he has a reason to get up and get moving. It is a big plus if his dog is an attention seeker who will demand such from his owner.

Over the last couple of decades, it has been shown that pets relieve the stress of those who lead busy lives. Owning a pet has been known to lessen the occurrence of heart attack and stroke.

Many single folks thrive on the companionship of a dog. Lifestyles are very different from a long time ago, and today more individuals seek the single life. However, they receive fulfillment from owning a dog.

Most likely the majority of our dogs live in family environments. The companionship they provide is well worth the effort involved. In my opinion, every child should have the opportunity to have a family dog. Dogs teach responsibility through understanding their care, feelings and even respecting their life cycles. Frequently those children who have not been exposed to dogs grow up afraid of dogs, which isn't good. Dogs sense timidity and some will take advantage of the situation.

Today more dogs are serving as service dogs. Since the origination of the Seeing Eye dogs years ago, we now have trained hearing dogs. Also dogs are trained to provide service for the handicapped and are able to perform many different tasks for their owners. Search and Rescue dogs, with their handlers, are sent throughout the world to assist in recovery of disaster victims. They are life savers.

Therapy dogs are very popular with nursing homes, and some hospitals even allow them to visit. The inhabitants truly look forward to their visits. They wanted and were allowed to have visiting dogs in their beds to hold and love.

Although some traits are inherited within a breed, every Chinese Crested is an individual with his own personality.

Nationally there is a Pet Awareness Week to educate

students and others about the value and basic care of our pets. Many countries take an even greater interest in their pets than Americans do. In those countries the pets are allowed to accompany their owners into restaurants and shops, etc. In the U.S. this freedom is only available to our service dogs. Even so we think very highly of the human/animal bond.

CANINE BEHAVIOR

Canine behavior problems are the number-one reason for pet owners to dispose of their dogs, either through new homes, humane shelters or euthanasia. Unfortunately there are too many owners who are unwilling to devote the necessary time to properly train their dogs. On the other hand, there are those who not only are concerned about inherited health problems but are also aware of the dog's mental stability.

You may realize that a breed and his group relatives (i.e., sporting, hounds, etc.) show tendencies to behavioral characteristics. An experienced breeder can acquaint you with his breed's personality. Unfortunately many breeds are labeled with poor temperaments when actually the breed as a whole is not affected but only a small percentage of individuals within the breed.

Inheritance and environment contribute to the dog's behavior. Some naïve people suggest inbreeding as the cause of bad temperaments. Inbreeding only results in poor behavior if the ancestors carry the trait. If there are excellent temperaments behind the dogs, then inbreeding will promote good temperaments in the offspring. Did you ever consider that inbreeding is what sets the characteristics of a breed? A purebred dog is the end result of inbreeding. This does not spare the mixed-breed dog from the same problems. Mixed-breed dogs frequently are the offspring of purebred dogs.

Not too many decades ago most of our dogs led a different lifestyle than what is prevalent today. Usually mom

Puppies need proper training and socialization from the very beginning to become welcomed and valued members of your household.

Good temperament is passed from parents to offspring. Your Chinese Crested breeder should carefully screen his dogs in order to produce the best possible puppies.

stayed home so the dog had human companionship and someone to discipline it if needed. Not much was expected from the dog. Today's mom works and everyone's life is at a much faster pace.

The dog may have to adjust to being a "weekend" dog. The family is gone all day during the week, and the dog is left to his own devices for entertainment. Some dogs sleep all day waiting for their family to come home and others become wigwam wreckers if given the opportunity. Crates do ensure the safety of the dog and the house. However, he could become a physically and emotionally cripple if he doesn't get enough exercise and attention. We still appreciate and want the companionship of our dogs although we expect more from them. In many cases we tend to forget dogs are just that—*dogs* not human beings.

Socializing and Training

Many prospective puppy buyers lack experience regarding the proper socialization and training needed to develop the type of pet we all desire. In the first 18 months, training does take some work. It is easier to start proper training before there is a problem that needs to be corrected.

The initial work begins with the breeder. The breeder should start socializing the puppy at five to six weeks of age and cannot let up. Human socializing is critical up through 12 weeks of age and likewise important during the following months. The litter should be left together during the first few weeks but it is necessary to separate them by ten weeks of age. Leaving them together after that time will increase competition for litter dominance. If puppies are not socialized with people by 12 weeks of age, they will be timid in later life.

Though all dogs are individuals, members of the same breed often tend toward similar behavior.

The eight- to ten-week age period is a fearful time for puppies. They need to be handled very gently around children and adults. There should be no harsh discipline during this time. Starting at 14 weeks of age, the puppy begins the juvenile period, which ends when he reaches sexual maturity around six to 14 months of age. During the juvenile period he needs to be introduced to strangers (adults, children and other dogs) on the home property. At sexual maturity he will begin to bark at strangers and become more protective. Males start to lift their legs to urinate but if you desire you can inhibit this behavior by walking your boy on leash away from trees, shrubs, fences, etc.

Teach your Chinese Crested how you want him to behave. Practice training and obedience exercises to further demonstrate your role as "alpha", the one in charge.

Perhaps you are thinking about an older puppy. You need to inquire about the puppy's social experience. If he has lived in a kennel, he may have a hard time adjusting to people and environmental stimuli. Assuming he has had a good social upbringing, there are advantages to an older puppy.

Training includes puppy kindergarten and a minimum of one to two basic training classes. During these classes you will learn how to dominate your youngster. This is especially important if you own a large breed of dog. It is somewhat harder, if not nearly impossible, for some owners to be the Alpha figure when their dog towers over them. You will be taught how to properly restrain your dog. This concept is important. Again it puts you in the Alpha position. All dogs need to be restrained many times during their lives. Believe it or not, some of our worst offenders are the eight-week-old puppies that are brought to our clinic. They need to be gently restrained for a nail trim but

the way they carry on you would think we were killing them. In comparison, their vaccination is a "piece of cake." When we ask dogs to do something that is not agreeable to them, then their worst comes out. Life will be easier for your dog if you expose him at a young age to the necessities of life— proper behavior and restraint.

UNDERSTANDING THE DOG'S LANGUAGE

Most authorities agree that the dog is a descendent of the wolf. The dog and wolf have similar traits. For instance both are pack oriented and prefer not to be isolated for long periods of time. Another characteristic is that the dog, like the wolf, looks to the leader—Alpha—for direction. Both the wolf and the dog communicate through body language, not only within their pack but with outsiders.

To be properly socialized, your Chinese Crested should meet as many different people as possible while growing up.

Every pack has an Alpha figure. The dog looks to you, or should look to you, to be that leader. If your dog doesn't receive the proper training and guidance, he very well may replace you as Alpha. This would be a serious problem and is certainly a disservice to your dog.

Eye contact is one way the Alpha wolf keeps order within his pack. You are Alpha so you must establish eye contact with your puppy. Obviously your puppy will have to look at you. Practice eye contact even if you need to hold his head for five to ten seconds at a time. You can give him a treat as a reward. Make sure your eye contact is gentle and not threatening. Later, if he has been naughty, it is permissible to give him a long, penetrating look. There are some older dogs that never learned eye contact as puppies and cannot accept eye contact. You should avoid eye contact with these dogs since they feel threatened and will retaliate as such.

Well-socialized Chinese Cresteds should be able to play with each other without showing fear or aggression.

Body Language

The play bow, when the forequarters are down and the hindquarters are elevated, is an invitation to play. Puppies play fight, which helps them learn the acceptable limits of biting. This is necessary for later in their lives.

Nevertheless, an owner may be falsely reassured by the playful nature of his dog's aggression. Playful aggression toward another dog or human may be an indication of serious aggression in the future. Owners should never play fight or play tug-of-war with any dog that is inclined to be dominant.

Signs of submission are:

1. Avoids eye contact.
2. Active submission—the dog crouches down, ears back and the tail is lowered.
3. Passive submission—the dog rolls on his side with his hindlegs in the air and frequently urinates.

Signs of dominance are:

1. Makes eye contact.
2. Stands with ears up, tail up and the hair raised on his neck.
3. Shows dominance over another dog by standing at right angles over it.

Dominant dogs tend to behave in characteristic ways such as:

1. The dog may be unwilling to move from his place (i.e., reluctant to give up the sofa if the owner wants to sit there).
2. He may not part with toys or objects in his mouth and may show possessiveness with his food bowl.
3. He may not respond quickly to commands.
4. He may be disagreeable for grooming and dislikes to be petted.

Dogs are popular because of their sociable nature. Those that have contact with humans during the first 12 weeks of life regard them as a member of their own species—their pack. All dogs have the potential for both dominant and submissive behavior. Only through experience and training do they learn to whom it is appropriate to show which behavior. Not all dogs are concerned with dominance but owners need to be aware of that potential. It is wise for the owner to establish his dominance early on.

A human can express dominance or submission toward a dog in the following ways:

1. Meeting the dog's gaze signals dominance. Averting the gaze signals submission. If the dog growls or threatens, averting the gaze is the first avoiding action to take—it may prevent attack. It is important to establish eye contact in the puppy. The older dog that has not been exposed to eye contact may see it as a threat and will not be willing to submit.

Some dogs will just nap during the day while everyone is out. Make sure it is safe for your Chinese Crested to wander the house when you are not there.

2. Being taller than the dog signals dominance; being lower signals submission. This is why, when attempting to make friends with a strange dog or catch the runaway, one should kneel down to his level. Some owners see their dogs become dominant when allowed on the furniture or on the bed. Then he is at the owner's level.

3. An owner can gain dominance by ignoring all the dog's social initiatives. The owner pays attention to the dog only when he obeys a command.

No dog should be allowed to achieve dominant status over any adult or child. Ways of preventing are as follows:

1. Handle the puppy gently, especially during the three- to four-month period.

2. Let the children and adults handfeed him and teach him to take food without lunging or grabbing.

3. Do not allow him to chase children or joggers.

4. Do not allow him to jump on people or mount their legs. Even females may be inclined to mount. It is not only a male habit.

5. Do not allow him to growl for any reason.

6. Don't participate in wrestling or tug-of-war games.

7. Don't physically punish puppies for aggressive behavior. Restrain him from repeating the infraction and

teach an alternative behavior. Dogs should earn everything they receive from their owners. This would include sitting to receive petting or treats, sitting before going out the door and sitting to receive the collar and leash. These types of exercises reinforce the owner's dominance.

Young children should never be left alone with a dog. It is important that children learn some basic obedience commands so they have some control over the dog. They will gain the respect of their dog.

FEAR

One of the most common problems dogs experience is being fearful. Some dogs are more afraid than others. On the lesser side, which is sometimes humorous to watch, dogs can be afraid of a strange object. They act silly when something is out of place in the house. We call his problem perceptive intelligence. He realizes the abnormal within his known environment. He does not react the same way in strange environments since he does not know what is normal.

A fearful Chinese Crested will be impossible to groom. Accustom your pet to the grooming process while young so that these tasks are easily accomplished as an adult.

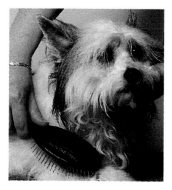

On the more serious side is a fear of people. This can result in backing off, seeking his own space and saying "leave me alone" or it can result in an aggressive behavior that may lead to challenging the person. Respect that the dog wants to be left alone and give him time to come forward. If you approach the cornered dog, he may resort to snapping. If you leave him alone, he may decide to come forward, which should be rewarded with a treat.

Some dogs may initially be too fearful to take treats. In these cases it is helpful to make sure the dog hasn't eaten for about 24 hours. Being a little hungry encourages him to accept the treats, especially if they are of the "gourmet" variety.

By being aware of your Chinese Crested's actions and reinforcing good behavior (and correcting bad behavior), you will both enjoy a happy and loving relationship.

Dogs can be afraid of numerous things, including loud noises and thunderstorms. Invariably the owner rewards (by comforting) the dog when it shows signs of fearfulness. When your dog is frightened, direct his attention to something else and act happy. Don't dwell on his fright.

AGGRESSION

Some different types of aggression are: predatory, defensive, dominance, possessive, protective, fear induced, noise provoked, "rage" syndrome (unprovoked aggression), maternal and aggression directed toward other dogs. Aggression is the most common behavioral problem encountered. Protective breeds are expected to be more aggressive than others but with the proper upbringing they can make very dependable companions. You need to be able to read your dog.

Many factors contribute to aggression including genetics and environment. An improper environment, which may include the living conditions, lack of social life, excessive punishment, being attacked or frightened by an aggressive dog, etc., can all influence a dog's behavior. Even spoiling him and giving too much praise may be detrimental. Isolation and the lack of human contact or exposure to frequent teasing by children or adults also can ruin a good dog.

Lack of direction, fear, or confusion lead to aggression in those dogs that are so inclined. Any obedience exercise, even the sit and down, can direct the dog and overcome fear and/or confusion. Every dog should learn these commands as a youngster, and there should be periodic reinforcement.

When a dog is showing signs of aggression, you should speak calmly (no screaming or hysterics) and firmly give a command that he understands, such as the sit. As soon as your dog obeys, you have assumed your dominant position. Aggression presents a problem because there may be danger to others. Sometimes it is an emotional issue. Owners may consciously or unconsciously encourage their dog's aggression.

If you have done everything according to "the book" regarding training and socializing and are still having a behavior problem, don't procrastinate. If your veterinarian isn't able to help, he should refer you to a behaviorist.

The Chinese Crested is popular as a pet because he is highly trainable and makes a great companion.

SUGGESTED READING

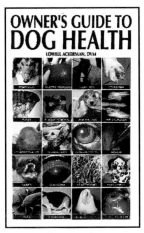

TS-214
Skin & Coat Care For
Your Dog
432 pages, over 300
full-color photos.

TS-249
Owner's Guide to Dog
Health
224 pages, over 190
full-color photos.

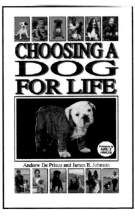

TS-252
Dog Behavior and Training
292 pages, over 200
full-color photos.

TS-257
Choosing A Dog for Life
384 pages, over 700
full-color photos.

INDEX